Read & Understand

Grade 6+

WITH LEVELED TEXTS

Mrs. Winters
Room 211

Writing: Delana Heidrich
Kathy Mattenklodt
Kathleen Simpson
Tekla White
Content Editing: Barbara Allman
De Gibbs
Camille Liscinsky
Art Direction: Cheryl Puckett
Cover Design: Liliana Potigian
Illustration: Judith Soderquist-Cummins
Design/Production: Yuki Meyer
John D. Williams

EMC 3446

Visit
teaching-standards.com
to view a correlation
of this book.
This is a free service.

Correlated to State and Common Core State Standards

Congratulations on your purchase of some of the finest teaching materials in the world.

For information about other Evan-Moor products, call 1-800-777-4362, fax 1-800-777-4332, or visit our Web site, www.evan-moor.com.

18 Lower Ragsdale Drive, Monterey, CA 93940-5746. Printed in USA.

CPSIA: Printed by McNaughton & Gunn, Saline, MI USA. [7/2012]

Contents

How to Use This Book

The Stories

The stories in this book include fiction, realistic fiction, historical fiction, nonfiction, biographies, and folk tales. With Lexile® scores ranging from 800 to 1100, the reading levels span mid-fifth grade through eighth grade.

Select a Story

Before selecting a story, determine how you will use the story.
Each story can be used

- as a directed lesson, with either an individual student or a group of students reading at the same level;
- by partners reading together; or
- for independent reading practice in the classroom or at home.

Preview the Story

1. Reproduce the story and give a copy to each student.
2. Discuss any vocabulary that might be difficult to decode or understand.
3. Have the students think about the title of the story and look at the picture or pictures to help them predict what the story is about.
4. Help students relate their prior knowledge and experience to the story.

Read the Story

A single story can be read for more than one purpose. You might first read the story for instructional purposes, and then have partners read the story again to improve comprehension and fluency. At a later time, you can use the story for independent reading. Each purpose calls for a different degree of story difficulty.

The Skill Pages

The four pages of reproducible activities that follow each story cover a variety of essential reading skills. The Skills Chart on page 5 provides an overview of the skills practiced in the activities. Each activity is suitable for either group instruction or independent practice.

Group Instruction

1. Reproduce the activity page for each student.
2. Make a transparency of the activity or write its content on the board.
3. Introduce the skill and guide students through the lesson.
4. Have students complete the activity as the group works through the lesson.

Independent Practice

Although many students will read the same story, they may each need to practice different skills. Assign the activities that are the most appropriate for each student's needs.

1. Be sure that the activity practices skills that have already been introduced to the student.
2. Review the directions and be sure that the student understands the task.
3. Go over the completed assignment with the student to assess his or her need for further practice.

Skills Chart

Stories / Skills	Recalling information	Main idea/details	Inferring/drawing conclusions	Critical/creative thinking	Compare/contrast	Summarizing/generalizing	Organizing information	Problems/solutions	Fact/opinion	Cause/effect	Similes/metaphors/imagery	Building vocabulary	Prefixes/suffixes/root words	Synonyms/antonyms	Parts of speech	Applying related knowledge	Exaggeration	Point of view	Genre study	Creative writing	Writing/personal narrative
The Fox and the Crow	•		•	•								•	•	•					•		
Japanese Celebrations	•			•	•							•	•		•						
Runner-Up	•											•			•					•	
Belling the Cat	•		•	•								•						•		•	
Hooray for Weeds!	•		•	•					•			•		•							
Marian Anderson	•		•				•					•									
Journey North	•		•	•		•	•					•			•						
City of Mystery	•		•	•								•	•								•
Nancy Lopez and Family	•				•					•		•				•					•
Iggie	•		•			•	•					•			•						
Justice for All	•		•	•			•	•				•				•					•
Animal Skyscrapers	•	•					•					•		•	•						
Two Sisters	•		•	•	•							•									
Indiana Sundays	•		•	•							•	•									
America's First Lady of Courage	•		•	•	•							•	•			•					•
The Day Pecos Bill Rode Old Twister	•				•						•	•					•				
Picturing History	•		•	•	•		•	•				•									•
Jackie Robinson	•	•	•	•	•		•					•									
Love That Chocolate!	•	•	•	•			•					•			•					•	
Laurence Yep	•		•	•		•						•							•	•	•
Let's Celebrate	•				•							•		•	•	•					

The Fox and the Crow

An Adapted Fable

The crow ruffled his feathers and strutted up and down on the branch of his favorite tree. It was dinnertime, but no berries, bugs, or worms would do for this crow. The other crows could eat that common food. This crow was a clever thief, and he had decided to steal a special delicacy for dinner.

The crow flew from the branch, circled over a nearby farm, and then landed near the barn. Inside the barn, on a shelf, were bricks of aging cheese. The crow pranced around the cheeses, eyeing each brick and, every now and then, stopping to peck at one. When he had almost reached the last brick, the crow finally found the perfect flavor.

The crow looked around and listened to make sure he was alone. The farmer was milking a cow in another part of the barn, and the farmer's wife was singing in the kitchen, so the crow boldly pulled off a large piece of the cheese. Hearing the noise from the crow's flapping wings, the farmer came running. He chased after the crow, waving his arms and shouting, but the crow flew above the trees in the orchard, and the farmer couldn't catch him.

The crow flew back to his branch. It wouldn't do to eat such a treat right away. He would wait until the rest of the flock returned so they could envy his tasty treasure. They would be back soon, arguing about which of them had found the most bugs and worms in the farmer's freshly plowed field, and it would be worth the wait to show off the cheese and devour it in front of them.

From her hiding place in a nearby thicket, a hungry fox spied the crow.

"I shall have that tasty morsel for myself," she declared. "It would be a shame for such a treat to be wasted on a crow. Besides, that bird thinks too well of himself. I've heard him boast about his skill as a thief to all the creatures in the forest. It will be easy to take his dinner away. Then let's see how much boasting he does."

The fox crept out of the thicket and sat under the crow's branch. She looked up and smiled, showing all her teeth.

"Ah, dear crow," she said, "I see that you have outfoxed the farmer again. I have never encountered a thief as clever as you are. We foxes are thought to be the wiliest animals on earth, but we can claim that title no longer. You, dear crow, are far more cunning than the sliest of us."

The crow moved his head from side to side, showing off the cheese.

"And you are as handsome as you are clever, friend crow," the fox continued. "Your feathers glisten in the sunlight. I see iridescent shades of green and a rainbow of colors dancing on your wings, and your eyes sparkle like jewels. How I would love to replace my feet with yours so I could perch on a tree branch and watch the world below me. There is no creature in the forest that can compare to you."

The crow flapped his wings and looked down at the fox.

"Believe me, dear crow," the fox went on, "I cannot praise you enough. And I can see that you know I am being truthful. Many animals say that the voice of the crow is the most unpleasant sound they have ever heard, but indeed, they are mistaken. How could any animal as handsome and as talented as you are make unpleasant sounds?"

The crow nodded in agreement.

"I don't wish to interrupt your dinner," said the fox, "not for one minute, but as a favor to this poor fox who will never be able to imitate your soothing, melodious tones, please sing a few notes. Every creature in the forest will enjoy your musical talent. You could serenade us with a long concert or enrich our lives with a trilling lullaby. I foresee a great musical future for you."

The crow was pleased to hear the fox's flattering remarks.

"Well?" asked the fox. "Will you sing for us, dear crow?"

"How can I refuse such a great admirer as the fox?" thought the crow.

As the crow opened his beak to sing the first caw, his piece of cheese fell to the ground, and the fox gobbled it up. Then the sad, hungry crow watched the fox disappear into the thicket.

Name ___________________________

Questions About *The Fox and the Crow*

1. Why didn't the crow want to eat berries, bugs, or worms?

____

2. The fable calls the crow "a clever thief." Do you agree or disagree? Use details from the story to support your opinion.

____

____

____

3. Did the fox like the crow? Explain why or why not.

____

____

____

4. List three things the crow did in the story that showed he was conceited, or vain.

____

____

____

5. Why did the crow drop the cheese?

____

6. What is another way that the fox could have gotten the crow to open his mouth?

____

____

____

Name ______________________

Vocabulary

Write the number of each word next to the correct definition.

1. envy	______	having a shiny array of shifting, rainbowlike colors
2. interrupt	______	to poke or jab in quick movements with a beak
3. morsel	______	to eat quickly and eagerly
4. delicacy	______	to stop an activity that is in progress
5. peck	______	walked in a swaggering or conceited way
6. thicket	______	to want someone else's good fortune for yourself
7. devour	______	a rare or special kind of food
8. strutted	______	a dense group of bushes or small trees
9. iridescent	______	disturbed the smoothness
10. ruffled	______	a small piece of food

Synonyms

1. Write each word listed below on the line next to its synonym.

imitate	glisten	pranced	melodious
serenade	boast	spied	common

copy	______________	ordinary	______________
spotted	______________	brag	______________
musical	______________	sing	______________
glitter	______________	danced	______________

2. List three synonyms that the fox uses in the story to describe how **clever** the crow is.

______________ ______________ ______________

Name ______________________

The Fox and the Crow

Prefixes

1. Add one of the following prefixes to each root word below to make a word that can be found in the story. Then use the meaning of the root word and the meaning of the prefix to write a definition for the new word.

dis	not; opposite	**mis**	wrong; bad or badly
en	to make or cause to be	**re**	again; back or backward
fore	earlier; in advance; in front of	**un**	not; opposite of or contrary
im, **in**	no; not; without		

a. appear ______________

____

b. place ______________

____

c. see ______________

____

d. taken ______________

____

e. rich ______________

____

2. Circle the underlined word in each sentence that correctly answers the question.

a. Was the fox patient or impatient while she was talking to the crow?

b. Was the fox polite or impolite to the crow?

c. Do many animals say that a crow makes pleasant or unpleasant sounds?

d. Was the crow pleased or displeased with the fox's remarks?

e. Did the crow want to eat foods that are common or uncommon for birds?

f. Did the fox tell the crow that he was comparable or incomparable to other creatures in the forest?

Name ______________________

What Makes It a Fable?

A **fable** is a story that teaches a moral, or lesson. The main characters are animals that have human traits, and one of the characters usually has a weakness, or flaw. The main action, or plot, of a fable is about a conflict, or problem, between the characters.

Answer the following questions about *The Fox and the Crow* to tell why it is a fable.

1. What human traits does the fox have?

____

2. What human traits does the crow have?

____

3. Which character has a flaw? What is the flaw?

____

4. What is the conflict, or problem, in the story?

____

5. What is the moral of the story?

____

True or False?

Flattery is false or insincere praise. The fox uses flattery to get the crow to drop the cheese. Find five examples of flattery in the story and write them on the lines below.

____

____

____

____

____

Japanese Celebrations

During every month of the year in Japan, there are festivals and special days to celebrate. Some Japanese celebrations are hundreds of years old, and many of them are just for children.

Shichi-Go-San

The English translation of *shichi-go-san* is *seven-five-three*. The Japanese festival Shichi-Go-San, celebrated on November 15, honors seven-, five-, and three-year-old children. On this special day, families visit a religious shrine to pray for the good health and happiness of the children. The day's celebration also includes parties and presents for the children. The children are given bags of holiday candy and are told that eating the candy will bring them good luck and a long life.

Children's Day

Although originally called Boys' Day, this national holiday now honors all Japanese children. Many Children's Day traditions, however, are still just for the boys in the family. On May 5, at the beginning of the day, families often take a special bath to wash away bad luck, and placing iris leaves in the water is thought to bring strength and bravery. Families also set up displays that include figures of warriors, toy weapons, banners, and armor for everyone to admire. Some of the weapons and armor in the displays are very old. Fathers often pass down their displays to their sons.

Brightly colored carp kites can be seen flying from poles in front of the houses of families that have sons. The large kite at the top symbolizes the father. The next kite represents the mother, and the last kite is for the son. More kites are added if the family has more sons. The carp is a strong, courageous fish that swims upstream against a river's currents. Japanese parents hope that their sons will grow to be strong and courageous like the carp.

Hina Matsuri

Hina Matsuri is a doll festival. Also called Girls' Day, it is celebrated every year on March 3. On this day, girls display a special set of dolls called *hina* (**hee**-na). Mothers and grandmothers often give their own sets of dolls to their young daughters or granddaughters, so many doll collections are old and valuable. Older dolls have painted porcelain faces and glass eyes. Most of the newer dolls are made of plastic.

The dolls include figures of the emperor and empress, ladies-in-waiting, the minister of state, courtiers, and court musicians, all dressed in traditional clothing. They are displayed on a tiered stand that is usually covered with a red cloth and are often placed amidst special furniture and replicas of food. After the holiday, the dolls are carefully stored away for the following year.

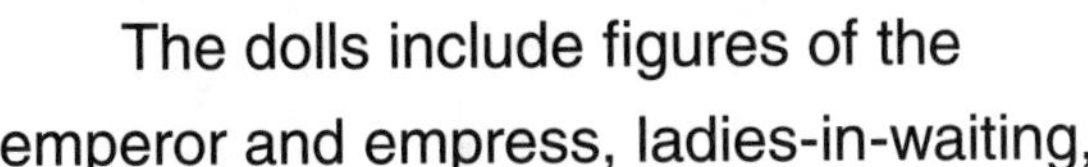

The Gion Festival

In 869, the Japanese city of Kyoto experienced a terrible epidemic during which many people became ill and many died. The emperor prayed to the gods for his people's health and sent an offering of weapons to the Gion Shrine. When his prayers were answered and people were no longer suffering from the disease, the thankful emperor organized a big parade to celebrate the first Gion Festival.

Today, huge decorated boxes, called *hoko,* are paraded through the streets. Some of the boxes weigh many tons, and they can be as tall as a four-story building. Some are hundreds of years old. The boxes are set on huge wheels that are about 8 feet (2.5 meters) in diameter. After the parade, they are taken apart and carefully stored for the next festival.

Each year before the Gion Festival, a boy is selected for a special role. Dressed up like a priest, with his face painted white, the boy inspects the boxes while they are being put together. Someone walks with the boy and holds an umbrella over his head to shade him from the sun. Then, right before the parade, the boy takes a place of honor on top of a hoko. As the hoko is pulled along the parade route, the boy has a bird's-eye view of the celebration.

New Year's Day

Greeting cards and family visits are New Year's traditions in Japan. The New Year celebration is on January 1. For Japanese children, the New Year celebration includes playing traditional games. Girls often play a game similar to badminton. Boys fly kites and spin tops. Both girls and boys buy strips of paper that have fortunes written on them. They tie the strips like blossoms onto the branches of bare winter trees. The children hope that this tradition will bring them good luck in the new year.

Tanabata

The Japanese Star Festival known as Tanabata is celebrated on the seventh day of the seventh month. It is the custom on this day for people, especially children, to write their wishes on small pieces of paper and hang them on bamboo branches. Some wishes are written in the form of poems. The bamboo branches may also be adorned with brightly colored paper decorations. Colorful paper streamers decorating the doorways of shops, schools, and homes are another common sight during the Tanabata festival.

The Sapporo Snow Festival

The whole family enjoys the weeklong Snow Festival in the city of Sapporo, which is in the northernmost part of Japan. Held each year in February, this festival is one of Japan's biggest winter events. Millions of people come to enjoy the winter activities and regional foods, but the highlights of the festival are the snow and ice sculptures. Teams of artists come to compete in an international snow sculpture contest. Hundreds of sculptures of famous people, buildings, and events are constructed each year. Some of the sculptures are more than 60 feet (18 m) tall!

Name ______________________________

Questions About *Japanese Celebrations*

1. Why do you think that Boys' Day is no longer just for boys?

____

____

2. Why did the emperor organize a parade to celebrate the first Gion Festival?

____

____

3. Write the letter of the correct Japanese celebration on the line next to each activity.

a. New Year's Day	b. Gion Festival	c. Children's Day
d. Shichi-Go-San	e. Hina Matsuri	f. Tanabata

_______ Carp kites fly from poles in front of houses.

_______ Huge decorated boxes are paraded through the streets.

_______ Young girls display special doll collections.

_______ Children play traditional games.

_______ A special bath washes away bad luck.

_______ A boy dressed up like a priest has a place of honor in the parade.

_______ Children write out their wishes and hang them on bamboo branches.

_______ Children go to parties and receive presents and bags of holiday candy.

4. Which Japanese festival would you like to attend? Explain why.

____

____

____

____

Name ______________________

Vocabulary

1. Write the letter of each word next to the correct definition.

a. badminton	______	having several levels or rows, one above the other
b. diameter	______	a type of fish
c. shrine	______	figures carved out of rock or another hard material
d. carp	______	referring to the fine clay used to make china objects
e. current	______	royal attendants
f. porcelain	______	decorated with ornaments
g. epidemic	______	a religious minister
h. adorned	______	a place or an area that honors a holy person or an event
i. courtiers	______	a game using rackets to hit a shuttlecock over a net
j. sculptures	______	the flow of water in a stream or river
k. priest	______	the spread of a disease affecting a lot of people
l. tiered	______	the measurement of a circle from one side to the other

2. Use your own words to explain the meaning of the phrase *bird's-eye view.*

____

3. The words *display* and *parade* are both used in the story as a noun and as a verb. Write your own sentence for each of these words. Then circle **noun** or **verb** to show how you used the word in the sentence.

display **noun** **verb**

____

____

parade **noun** **verb**

____

____

Name ____________________

Root Words and Suffixes

1. Write the root word and the suffix for each word listed below. Remember that some words may have a spelling change.

	Root Word	Suffix
a. celebration	________	________
b. happiness	________	________
c. symbolize	________	________
d. brightly	________	________
e. courageous	________	________
f. Japanese	________	________
g. valuable	________	________
h. musician	________	________
i. thankful	________	________

2. Write each suffix listed above on the line next to its meaning.

a. having or full of ________
b. deserving or worthy of ________
c. condition or quality of ________
d. of a place ________
e. make into ________
f. in a certain way ________
g. person ________
h. the state or act of ________
i. having the quality of ________

Bonus: Use the meanings of the suffixes above to write a definition for the word **carefully**.

____

____

Name ______________________

Using Adjectives

1. Circle all of the adjectives in each of the following sentences.

   a. They are displayed on a tiered stand covered with a red cloth and are often placed amidst special furniture and replicas of food.

   b. Greeting cards and family visits are New Year's traditions in Japan, and, for Japanese children, traditional games are part of the celebration.

   c. Some wishes are written in the form of poems, and the bamboo branches may also be adorned with colorful paper decorations.

2. Find the adjectives or adjective phrases in the story that describe the items below and write them on the lines.

   a. ______________, ______________ fish

   b. ______________ ______________ carp kites

   c. ______________ ______________ faces

   d. ______________ ______________ boxes

   e. ______________ ______________ trees

   f. ______________ and ______________ sculptures

3. Write adjectives of your own to describe each item below.

   a. ______________ ______________ tower

   b. ______________ ______________ meadow

   c. ______________ ______________ bicycle

   d. ______________ ______________ sweater

   e. ______________ ______________ vase

Runner-Up

Zach checked the laces on his running shoes and then began stretching his hamstrings. He glanced at Jordan, two lanes over. Jordan had won every race he'd ever entered, but in Bennington's meet against Elmhurst last spring, Zach came in only two seconds behind him. "Jordan isn't going to win this time," Zach thought. "I've cut at least three seconds off my time since the Elmhurst meet."

Today wasn't a meet or anything like that, but it was an important practice. The coach would be making up his mind about which runners should be in which events this season. Bennington's first meet was just two weeks away, and Zach had been training hard. His granddad would be coming from Wisconsin to see him race. Grandpa Morgan had been a track star himself. He had won lots of medals and even ran in the Olympics. He was always telling his friends about his grandson Zach and how Zach would run in the Olympics, too, someday. Knowing that Grandpa Morgan would be watching him made winning more important than ever to Zach. Coming in second just wouldn't be good enough. Besides, he had told his granddad that he was the best runner on the team.

The flag went down, and Zach flew around the track. He was out in front, exactly where he wanted to be. At the halfway mark, he felt someone moving up behind him, but no one passed him. Three-quarters of the way to the finish line, Zach felt someone pushing for the lead again. It has to be Jordan, he thought. Zach had pressed so hard to be in front that he didn't have enough energy left to hold the lead if another runner challenged him. So far, however, no one was passing him. Zach's body ached, but he didn't slow down. He knew he had to hold on. Suddenly, the other runner made his move, crossing the finish line just ahead of Zach.

Wiping his face with a damp towel, Zach headed for the bleachers.

"Whoa," said a voice behind him. "Great race, buddy. Thanks for tiring out the other runners with that fast start. It made winning a lot easier for me."

Zach turned to see Jordan grinning at him.

"Save a little speed for the last half," Jordan continued. "Then, next time, maybe you'll finish ahead of me—if I'm not so far out in front you can't catch me, that is."

Zach felt angry, but he tried not to show it. Whenever Jordan wins, Zach thought, he always has to rub it in and tell me how I should have run. Worse than that, however, Zach knew that Jordan was right. If he had just paced himself and held back a little at the beginning, Zach knew he could have ended with a burst of speed and won.

"Thanks," Zach said to Jordan when he had his breath and his temper under control. "I'll keep that in mind."

The other runners began crowding around Jordan, and for the first time, Zach was glad that Jordan was the center of attention. Their conversation was over, so now he wouldn't have to congratulate Jordan on running a great race.

For the next two weeks, Zach tried holding back on the track, but it just didn't work for him. He either had to be ahead at the beginning of the race or found himself lagging behind for the whole race.

"Don't worry about it, Zach, buddy," Jordan kept reminding him. "I can coast in just fine this way. And if we take first and second, we'll put more points on the board for Bennington."

The coach put both Jordan and Zach on the relay team. "Keep it fast," the coach told them, "but not so fast that you use up your energy for the big race. With both of you on the team, just think of it as a warm-up. Zach, watch how Jordan handles it. He was on the relay team last year. Remember, we need the points, not a record."

Zach liked running more than anything, although he often thought that he'd like it even more without Jordan around. Grandpa Morgan always told him that the great thing about running is you're competing with yourself. You keep trying to better your own record each time. Zach guessed that Grandpa Morgan never had to worry about anyone like Jordan. Actually, Grandpa Morgan was just like Jordan—the one who always came in first.

The morning after Grandpa Morgan arrived from Wisconsin, he and Zach went running before Zach left for school. He told Zach about some of his races and about the Olympics.

"Maybe you should finish your last two years of high school in Wisconsin," he told Zach. "I know a great coach—me! I'll have you ready for college and the Olympics by the time you graduate."

Zach wanted to run in the Olympics, but would his granddad still think he was good enough if he saw Jordan come in first at the meet? On the day of the meet, Zach and his granddad were up before anyone else. As they ate breakfast, Grandpa Morgan talked about nothing but running.

"Gramps," Zach interrupted, "I have to tell you something."

For the past week, Zach had thought about what he should say to his grandfather. He finally decided to tell the truth even if it meant that Grandpa Morgan wouldn't have anything more to do with him.

"I'm not the best runner on the team," Zach blurted out. "I know I talk like I am sometimes, but Jordan has never lost the mile, and I'm not as good as you were."

"There's only one sure thing about running, Zach," Grandpa Morgan replied. "No matter how fast your feet fly, there's always someone who can cross the finish line in front of you. I won lots of races, but I lost some, too. I ran in the Olympics, but I don't have any Olympic medals. Sure, I hope you'll take up where I left off, if that's what you want. But even if you come in next to last, you're still the greatest grandkid I could ever have."

"You know, Zach," Grandpa Morgan continued, "running was my whole life for so long that I don't have much else to talk about. It's time I stopped talking about running and learned about some other things. After the meet, let's go somewhere for dinner, and you can tell me what else is going on in your life. Maybe we should take in a movie, too!"

Questions About *Runner-Up*

1. How did Zach feel about Jordan? Explain your answer.

2. Why was Zach always losing to Jordan?

3. Why did Zach think it was more important than ever to win the race at the first track meet this year?

4. What did Grandpa Morgan think was the great thing about running?

5. What did Grandpa Morgan tell Zach was the only sure thing about running?

6. After Zach told the truth, how did Grandpa Morgan's attitude about running seem to change? Why do you think his attitude changed?

Name ________________________

Runner-Up

Related Words

Many words take on different forms with related meanings. Read the definitions for each set of related words below. Then write the correct word on the line to complete each sentence.

1. **compete**—to go against one or more opponents to win or to be the best at something
   competitive—having a strong desire to win or succeed in a contest or competition
   competition—a struggle to win or to be the best at something; a contest
   competitor—a person or group competing against others in a contest; an opponent

   a. The winner of the state dance ________________ will win go on to ________________ in a national contest.

   b. Mark was a strong ________________ in our local bowling tournament.

   c. Mary is the most ________________ player on the school's softball team.

2. **challenge**—(n.) an invitation to take part in a contest; something that is difficult to accomplish successfully (v.) to invite opponents to compete
   challenger—the person who invites others to compete; a competitor
   challenging—difficult to accomplish successfully

   a. It was the most ________________ race Zach had ever run.

   b. Coming in first didn't seem much of a ________________ for Jordan.

   c. Mel's ________________ watched him warm up for the broad jump.

3. **congratulate**—to praise another's accomplishments
   congratulations—expressions of praise for another's performance or good fortune

   a. Our surprising victory earned ________________ from our opponents.

   b. Everyone gathered to ________________ the team's most valuable player.

4. **event**—a particular contest or activity or a part of a program
   eventful—having many events or occurrences

   a. Zach was picked to run in the relay ________________ at the track meet.

   b. Saturday was an ________________ day for Zach and his grandpa.

Name ______________________

Runner-Up

Multiple Meanings

A. Many words have more than one meaning. Write the letter of the correct meaning for the word in bold type on the line next to each sentence below.

a. reduced　　b. examined　　c. moving in front of
d. marked　　e. sliced　　f. meeting the minimum requirements

_______ The runners **checked** their shoelaces before the race.

_______ Kate **checked** each box correctly on the answer sheet for the exam.

_______ Zach had **cut** his finish time by three seconds since his last race.

_______ My mother **cut** her finger while she was peeling carrots.

_______ The runners were moving up behind Zach, but no one was **passing** him.

_______ Not a single student was **passing** Mr. Sadler's algebra class.

B. The same word can be used in different ways. Write **noun** or **verb** on the line after each sentence below to tell how the word in bold type is being used.

1. The first track **meet** of the season was two weeks away. _______________
2. Steve was anxious to **meet** his new roommate. _______________
3. Zach had to **press** hard to stay ahead of the other runners. _______________
4. The newspaper was ready to go to **press**. _______________
5. The coach told Zach to save his energy for the big **race**. _______________
6. Zach's grandfather came to see him **race**. _______________

C. Write two sentences for the word **record**. Use the word as a **noun** in the first sentence and as a **verb** in the second sentence.

1. ____

2. ____

Name ______________________

Runner-Up

Write Your Own Ending

Write a different ending for the story. Include what happened between Zach and Jordan during the race and how Zach felt about the results of the race.

Belling the Cat

An Adapted Fable

"Something must be done," said Percy, collapsing on the floor of his mouse house after charging through the hole in the wall. His tail had a nasty gash in it, and his body shook uncontrollably.

"You poor dear. It's the cat again, isn't it?" said his wife, Agatha, as she pulled Percy across the floor to their nest and covered him with a blanket.

"Indeed, it is!" said Percy. "He had his claws in my tail! I escaped by biting his paw. That fanged monster has caught me three times this week. I shudder to think what might happen to me, good wife. How will you and the children manage if the cat eats me?"

"Don't even mention that!" Agatha shrieked. "You must not take any more chances, and that's all there is to it."

"Then how will we eat?" asked Percy. "The cat hides in the kitchen and seems to hear every pawstep no matter how quiet. That fiendish feline had three of our friends for his snacks last week."

"It's so unfair," complained Agatha. "After seeing all the food that gets wasted around here, you'd surely think that the people in this house could share. Perhaps we could ask the farmer's wife to leave some of their scraps at our door. Then we wouldn't have to go into the kitchen or bother the cat."

"Good wife, you clearly do not understand the situation," Percy responded. "The people in this house are selfish, and they despise mice. When they moved in here, they brought the cat with them and have set traps everywhere to get rid of us. I know how to steer clear of the traps, but that cat is a sneaky and cruel creature that lurks in every nook and cranny and pounces on anything that moves. Honest, hardworking mice like us will never be safe as long as that cat continues to prowl this house."

“Well then,” said Agatha, “I suppose we must move. There must be a house or a barn or a store where we would be welcome. We are quite useful, I believe. After all, we do clean the floors of crumbs and scraps.”

“But even if we wanted to go out and find a safe place to call home, how would we get past the cat and out the door with our nest and all of our children?” asked Percy.

“For the life of me, dear husband, I can’t think of a way,” said Agatha.

“Then I will call a meeting of all the mice in the house,” said Percy. “If we discuss this problem sensibly, we will surely find a solution. We can travel inside the walls and meet in the bedroom closet without running into the cat.”

The next morning, Percy tapped out an SOS with his tail, and every mouse from the attic to the basement scurried between the walls to the big closet in the bedroom. Percy clapped his paws together for silence.

“We are all aware,” he began, “of the dangerous creature that lurks in this house, waiting to devour us. We also know that if it catches us, we will be tortured and killed. But if we stay safely hidden inside the walls, we will starve. We must, therefore, find a way to stop the creature. We must find a way to get past the cat!”

Before Percy could utter another word, there was a horrifying yowl and frantic scratching at the closet door. Sharp claws reached out from under the door, just barely missing Percy as he jumped away.

“Tomorrow! In the attic!” Percy squeaked as, one by one, the mice squeezed through the crack in the closet wall and scurried back to their nests. Percy was the last to leave. He scrambled through the crack just as the closet door swung open and the snarling cat charged in.

Percy and Agatha heard the farmer’s wife praising the cat. “Were you trying to catch more of those terrible mice that roam our house?” she asked. “You clever and wonderful cat. You’ve caught three mice already this week. In a month’s time, you’ll have done away with all the mice, won’t you? Just like you did in our last house.”

Percy peered through the crack and saw the farmer’s wife petting the cat as it purred and snuggled in her arms.

“How disgusting!” Percy said to his wife. “How could anyone be fond of a cat?”

The next morning, all the mice climbed inside the walls to the attic, and Percy began again.

"I have called you all here to discuss how we can save ourselves from the deadly and terrible cat and live, once more, without fear. If we leave our homes in this house, who knows what new dangers we will find. Furthermore, we would have to flee for our lives and leave all our possessions behind just to get out of here. Who has a solution to this problem?"

All the mice squeaked at once, telling stories about their encounters with the cat. Finally, Leah, one of the newest mouse residents, stood next to Percy and raised her paw for silence.

"The solution is simple," said Leah. "If we know where the cat is at all times, we can stay away from him. When I lived in a barn, the barn cat had a bell on her collar. We could always hear her coming and going so we could hide where she couldn't reach us. Surely, then, you see that all we have to do here is place a bell on this cat's collar."

"Why didn't I think of that?" said Percy. "A belled cat would be dangerous, but certainly not *as* dangerous. All in favor of placing a bell on the cat's collar, squeak 'yes.'"

Every mouse except Agatha squeaked with enthusiastic agreement.

"Very clever, indeed!" said Agatha. "Now which one of you brave mice will volunteer to place the bell on the cat's collar?"

Every mouse was silent.

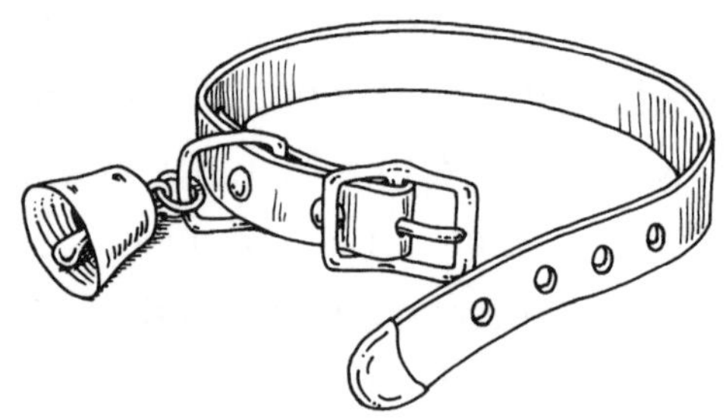

Name ______________________________

Questions About *Belling the Cat*

1. Percy and the other mice in the story are facing a dangerous dilemma.
   a. What might happen if the mice stay in the house?

   ____

   b. What might happen if they try to leave the house?

   ____

   ____

2. What are Agatha's two suggestions for staying away from the cat?

   ____

   ____

3. What does Percy think of Agatha's ideas?

   ____

   ____

4. How does Percy show leadership qualities?

   ____

   ____

5. Why does Percy change the location of the meeting place from the big closet to the attic?

   ____

   ____

6. Were you surprised at the way the mice responded to Leah's suggestion for avoiding the cat? Explain why or why not.

   ____

   ____

Name ______________________________

Belling the Cat

Vocabulary

A. Write each word listed below on the line next to its definition.

fiendish	feline	sensibly	shudder	prowl	utter
collapsing	lurks	gash	frantic	fond	fanged

1. ______________________ to roam around looking for prey
2. ______________________ a long, deep cut
3. ______________________ to speak or say
4. ______________________ falling down due to a sudden loss of strength
5. ______________________ like a devil or demon
6. ______________________ in a way that shows good judgment
7. ______________________ behaving wildly out of fear or distress
8. ______________________ any kind of cat
9. ______________________ feeling affection or love
10. ______________________ having long, pointed teeth
11. ______________________ sneaks around and stays hidden, waiting to attack
12. ______________________ to tremble with fear

B. Write a sentence for each of the words below. Make sure the sentence shows that you know what the word means. Use a dictionary if you need help.

despise   snarling   flee

1. ____

____

2. ____

____

3. ____

____

Name ______________________

Belling the Cat

Comparing Points of View

A character's opinion about or attitude toward someone or something in a story is called **point of view.**

1. Describe the problem in the story from the point of view of each character below.

   a. Percy: ______________________

   b. the farmer's wife: ______________________

   c. the cat: ______________________

2. Use point of view to help you draw conclusions about the characters that answer the questions below. Support your conclusions with details from the story.

   a. How does the cat feel about the farmer's wife?

   ____

   ____

   b. How does Percy feel about people?

   ____

   ____

   c. How does the farmer's wife feel about the cat?

   ____

   ____

3. Use point of view and details from the story to answer the following questions.

   a. Why did Leah think that her suggestion to bell the cat was a good solution?

   ____

   ____

   b. Did Agatha think that Leah's suggestion to bell the cat was a good solution? Why or why not?

   ____

   ____

Name ______________________________

Continue the Story

Use what you know about writing conversations to extend the meeting that the mice were having in the attic. Include how the mice respond to Agatha, what arguments are made for or against belling the cat, and another solution for the mice to consider.

Hooray for Weeds!

Weeds are the uninvited guests of the plant world. They sprout up in yards, gardens, forests, pastures, and even in the cracks of streets and sidewalks. They can put down roots in places where other plants can't grow at all. Gardeners don't like to see weeds, but weeds are important in many ways.

Like other green plants, weeds capture the energy of the sun and turn it into food. As the weeds absorb water, their roots pull in vitamins and minerals from the soil. When animals eat the roots or other parts of the weeds, they add needed nutrients to their diets. Muskrats take in nutritious vitamins and minerals when they eat cattails. Gophers and mice thrive on the tasty roots of many different weeds. The seeds and berries that some weeds produce are valuable food sources for insects, birds, and other animals. Even humans enjoy eating some kinds of weeds.

Both man and beast can eat all parts of common dandelions. This weed is rich in vitamins A and C and also contains important minerals. In spring, dandelion leaves can be picked and boiled to eat as a leafy green vegetable that tastes a little like spinach.

Dandelion

Before the buds open, the dandelion's yellow flowers can be picked and then roasted, and dandelion roots can be boiled to make tea. Rodents feed on dandelion roots, bees gather pollen and nectar from the flowers, and horses eat the leaves.

Like dandelion leaves, chickweed leaves can also be gathered and cooked like spinach. Although it is not welcome in lawns and gardens, chickweed is a nutritious plant.

Chickweed

Weeds can be sources of calcium, which is an important mineral for the healthy growth of bones and teeth. When an animal dies, its bones deposit calcium in the soil. The roots of weeds and other plants absorb the calcium. The plant you eat today might contain calcium that was in the skull of a saber-toothed tiger!

Weeds deposit calcium in the soil, too. As weeds die and decay, the calcium they have absorbed goes back into the soil. When soil is washed into a stream, river, or ocean, algae and other microscopic water plants absorb the calcium. Then fish eat the plants, and the people and other animals that eat the fish also benefit from the calcium.

Weeds help the soil in many ways. They loosen it with their roots so that insects and other animals can dig more easily. As dead weeds decay, bacteria and fungi in the soil break them down to form more soil. When fires destroy forests and grasslands, fast-growing weeds often sprout up to hold the soil in place until new trees grow. The roots of weeds, trees, and other plants hold rich topsoil in place so it won't be carried away by wind or heavy rains.

By holding the soil in place, weeds help prevent erosion and keep rivers and streams from becoming clogged with mud and chemicals. Fish and other animals that live in or near rivers and streams die when they don't have clean water. Sediment-choked rivers can flood fields, cause damage to food crops, and prevent hydroelectric power plants from operating properly—or at all!

The benefits of humble weeds don't stop with the soil either. Giant weeds may act as shields to slow strong winds. Prickly weeds, such as the thistle and the wild rose, shelter rabbits, birds, and other small animals. Hawks and large predators can't get through stickers, thorns, and brambles to find their prey.

Thistle

Weeds are very important to the plant and animal kingdoms and help make the world a better place to live. The next time you see dandelions, chickweed, thistles, cattails, poison ivy, or any other kinds of weeds, tell them "thanks" for a job well done or just say, "Hooray for weeds!"

Name ______________________

Questions About *Hooray for Weeds!*

1. Why are weeds considered to be nutritious?

____

2. How do people typically prepare the following dandelion parts for eating?

   a. flowers: ______________________

   b. leaves: ______________________

   c. roots: ______________________

3. How do some fish become a source of calcium for people and other animals?

____

____

____

4. How do weeds help prevent soil erosion?

____

____

5. Name three problems that may arise when erosion clogs rivers and streams with mud and chemicals.

____

____

____

6. Why might a farmer disagree with the title of this story?

____

____

____

Name ______________________________

Hooray for Weeds!

Vocabulary

A. Write the number of each word next to its definition.

1. nutrients	______	to place or set down
2. sprout	______	a mineral that helps build strong bones
3. calcium	______	the wearing away of soil
4. absorb	______	healthful; containing nutrients
5. deposit	______	to drink in or soak up
6. nutritious	______	the fine sand and soil at the bottoms of lakes and rivers
7. decay	______	to begin to grow
8. topsoil	______	to break down or decompose
9. sediment	______	vitamins and minerals
10. erosion	______	the layer of dirt at the ground's surface

B. Use words from the list above to complete the sentences below.

1. Decaying weeds ____________________ vitamins and other ____________________ into the soil.
2. The calcium that weeds ____________________ from the soil is passed on to the animals that eat the weeds.
3. The strong roots of fast-growing weeds help keep ____________________ from washing away.
4. Weeds are hardy plants that can ____________________ up in places where other plants can't grow.
5. Strong winds and heavy rains are natural causes of ____________________.
6. Too much ____________________ in rivers keeps them from flowing freely.
7. Algae absorbs ____________________ and other minerals from the soil that is washed into ponds and rivers.
8. As weeds ____________________, they break down to form more soil.

Name ______________________________

Synonyms and Antonyms

A. Read each pair of words below. Write **S** on the line if the words are **synonyms**. Write **A** on the line if the words are **antonyms**.

1. decay rot ______
2. thrive wither ______
3. capture release ______
4. nutritious healthful ______
5. uninvited welcome ______
6. soil dirt ______
7. benefit harm ______
8. shelter protect ______
9. clogged blocked ______
10. prickly smooth ______

B. Read each sentence below. Cross out the word that is wrong and write the antonym used in the story on the line to make the sentence read correctly.

1. Dandelions are uncommon weeds. ____________________
2. Algae are huge water plants found in ponds, rivers, and oceans. ____________________
3. Some weeds produce seeds and berries that are worthless sources of food for animals. ____________________
4. Sediment in rivers can cause floods that repair food crops. ____________________
5. The roots of weeds tighten the soil so that insects and other animals can dig more easily. ____________________
6. By holding the soil in place, weeds help cause erosion. ____________________

Name ____________________

Facts and Opinions

A nonfiction story contains **facts**, or information that can be proved. It may also contain **opinions**, which are beliefs that are supported or confirmed by facts.

A. Read each opinion below and write a fact from the story that supports the opinion.

1. **Opinion:** Weeds help make the world a better place to live.

   Fact: ____________________

2. **Opinion:** Weeds are the uninvited guests of the plant world.

   Fact: ____________________

3. **Opinion:** Humans enjoy eating weeds.

   Fact: ____________________

4. **Opinion:** Weeds help the soil.

   Fact: ____________________

5. **Opinion:** The benefits of weeds don't stop with the soil.

   Fact: ____________________

B. Write an opinion you have about weeds. Support your opinion with facts from the story.

____

Marian Anderson

1897–1993

In 1955, Marian Anderson became the first African American singer to perform in a major role at New York's Metropolitan Opera House.

Anderson began singing publicly at the age of six when she joined the junior choir at her church. After a few years, she was singing in both the junior and senior choirs. When visitors to the church heard Marian, they often invited the choirs to sing at their churches or to perform at special events.

Marian's parents knew she had a special gift for music, but they couldn't afford to pay for music lessons. Then, when Marian was twelve years old, her father died. Without him to support the family, Marian, her mother, and her two sisters moved in with her grandmother.

Anna Anderson, Marian's mother, did her best to support her daughters. She worked hard cleaning houses and washing and sewing clothes. Marian earned money singing sometimes. At first, she gave all the money to her mother. Later, she used some of it for music lessons.

Music was Anderson's favorite subject in school. During high school, she joined the Philadelphia Choral Society, which often sang in other cities. When she was out of town, she missed classes at school, but her teachers helped her make up her work.

Although already becoming well-known, Anderson knew that if she wanted to pursue a singing career, she would have to study music and take singing lessons. A voice teacher who lived nearby knew Marian's situation and started giving her lessons, usually at no charge. With this teacher's help, Anderson learned many new songs, as well as new ways to control her voice.

After high school, Anderson wanted to continue studying music. She tried to enroll in a Philadelphia music school, but when she went there to pick up an application, she was turned away because she was black. Throughout much of Anderson's life, many American schools and businesses discriminated against blacks and other minorities, and many public facilities were segregated.

When Marian was invited to Georgia to sing, she and her mother had to ride in a section of the train that was set aside for blacks, and they were not allowed to eat in the dining car. In New York and other cities, Anderson had to stay in hotels that were far from where she had been invited to sing because they were the only hotels that allowed blacks. But Anderson didn't let discrimination and segregation stand in her way.

Determined to make singing her career, Anderson continued taking voice lessons privately. Her church even raised money so she could study with a famous teacher. As Anderson's singing improved, she earned more money from her concerts, and in 1925, she won a competition to sing with the New York Philharmonic Orchestra.

In 1927, Anderson went to Europe to study music. She worked hard to learn foreign languages so she could sing songs written in those languages, especially the songs from European operas. She was invited to sing in Norway, Sweden, and Finland. Her concerts were always successful, and many famous European composers and musicians attended them. Her next trip to Europe lasted two years, and she sang in many other countries.

Now famous, both at home and abroad, Anderson was still not allowed to stay in some hotels or eat at many restaurants in the United States, and there were still auditoriums where she was not allowed to sing. She was once scheduled to sing at Constitution Hall in Washington, D.C., but the concert was canceled. African Americans were not allowed to perform there.

Learning that one of the country's greatest singers was not permitted to perform in the nation's capital made many people angry. The government finally invited Anderson to sing on the steps of the Lincoln Memorial, and on Easter Sunday, 1939, more than 75,000 people, black and white, sat together and listened to the concert. Later that year, Anderson was invited by President Franklin D. Roosevelt to sing at the White House.

In 1955, when she was 58 years old, Anderson became a regular company member of the New York Metropolitan Opera, but she was nowhere near the end of her career. In 1957, the U.S. State Department sent her on a concert tour throughout Southeast Asia. A year later, she was appointed as a member of the United Nations' American delegation.

Anderson continued to perform throughout the world until Easter Sunday, 1965, when, at Carnegie Hall in New York City, she gave her final public performance. Until her death in 1993, however, Anderson continued to receive public recognition for her music and for her work with people all over the world. Her voice and her courage were admired everywhere.

Name ______________________________

Questions About *Marian Anderson*

1. When did Marian Anderson first show a talent for singing?

   ____

2. How did voice lessons improve Anderson's natural talent?

   ____

3. How was Anderson's life in Europe different from her life in the United States?

   ____

   ____

   ____

4. Why was Anderson's concert at Constitution Hall canceled?

   ____

5. What was significant about Anderson's performance on the steps of the Lincoln Memorial?

   ____

   ____

6. Why do you think that Anderson was appointed to the United Nations' American delegation?

   ____

   ____

   ____

   ____

7. When and where did Marian Anderson give her final public performance?

   ____

Name ____________________

Marian Anderson

Vocabulary

Read the two definitions for each word below. Fill in the circle next to the meaning of the word as it was used in the story.

1. company
   Ⓐ a group of associated performers
   Ⓑ one or more guests or visitors
2. pursue
   Ⓐ to chase in order to catch
   Ⓑ to work at in order to achieve
3. minority
   Ⓐ the smaller of two groups within one large group
   Ⓑ a group of people that differ from the main population
4. discrimination
   Ⓐ the act of treating people unfairly for unjust reasons
   Ⓑ the act of seeing or distinguishing small differences
5. application
   Ⓐ a computer program for a specific task
   Ⓑ a written request to be chosen for or given something
6. competition
   Ⓐ a contest or match
   Ⓑ opposition or a rival for the same goal
7. recognition
   Ⓐ the act of remembering someone
   Ⓑ a tribute or praise
8. foreign
   Ⓐ unfamiliar or strange
   Ⓑ having to do with another country

Musical Word Search

Find each word listed in the word box and circle it in the puzzle.

Word Box

choir	orchestra
composer	performance
concert	singer
lessons	songs
musician	tour
opera	voice

v	m	u	s	i	c	i	a	n	o	w
o	h	a	t	v	l	e	t	e	r	t
p	e	r	f	o	r	m	a	n	c	e
e	t	r	c	i	j	g	w	r	h	a
r	s	t	o	c	c	u	e	l	e	m
a	o	h	m	e	o	g	r	e	s	n
o	c	r	p	h	n	s	o	s	t	e
n	e	s	o	i	c	b	o	s	r	h
p	m	a	s	r	e	c	k	o	a	i
v	o	l	e	s	r	s	o	n	g	s
t	o	u	r	c	t	r	e	s	m	e

Name ______________________________

Marian Anderson

Sequencing

A. Number the events in each part of Anderson's life chronologically.

Childhood and Adolescence

_______ began to earn money for her singing

_______ sang in the junior and senior church choirs

_______ sang in public when she was six years old

_______ joined a choral society and sang in other cities

_______ began singing lessons and learned to control her voice

Early Career

_______ scheduled concert canceled at Constitution Hall

_______ studied privately with a famous voice teacher

_______ not allowed to enroll in a Philadelphia music school

_______ studied music and languages in Europe

_______ won a singing competition

Later Success

_______ performed for over 75,000 people at the Lincoln Memorial

_______ joined the New York Metropolitan Opera

_______ invited to sing at the White House

_______ sent on a concert tour of Southeast Asia

_______ served as a member of the United Nations' American delegation

B. List, in chronological order, the three events in Anderson's life that you feel were the most important.

____

____

____

Name ___________________________

Character Map

Develop a character map for Marian Anderson. Write an adjective that describes one of Anderson's qualities or characteristics on the line at the top of each box. Then write one fact from the story in each box to support that characteristic.

Marian Anderson

Journey North

This letter might have been written by a young settler in early California.

April 10, 1781

Dear Grandfather,

As I write this letter, it is spring in the year 1781. More than five years have passed since our family left New Spain. I am sending this letter so you will know about our journey and what has happened to us. We know now that we will never be able to return to New Spain, and my parents have asked me to caution you and the others about joining us as we had agreed before we left. The journey by land is too dangerous, and even travel by sea would be difficult and very long.

We are grateful that we are all in good health. My youngest brother, Pedro, was born since we arrived in Alta California. My other six brothers and sisters are busy helping our parents. There is rich land here, but all that we have must be made or grown with our own hands. Since I am thirteen now, I am responsible for the fields and for taking care of the cattle while my father is guarding the mission and our community. The houses of the community lack even small comforts, and sailing ships seldom come this way with supplies.

I am able to send you this letter because I studied with Father Font, the Franciscan priest who accompanied us on the trip north. Learning to read and write during those difficult days gave me hope. Our leader, Juan Bautista de Anza, kept our caravan moving in spite of hardships that you cannot imagine. He cared for those who became ill and gave cheer when our spirits and our faith failed us. Without him, we would have perished before reaching Alta California.

Traveling with mules and cattle proved to be a challenge for our families. It was a major task to organize our caravan every day before we set out, and we had to find food and water for the animals all along the way. We had to stop many days so that the animals could eat and rest.

During the first few days of the trip, everyone was in good spirits, even though our progress was very slow. The hot summer days had passed, but the area was windy and unpleasant, and the desert provided little water and grass for our animals. After a month, we reached the camp of a Pima chief on the banks of the Colorado River. The cold, bitter winter had made fording the river impossible. Many of us had never seen such a wide river and such rushing water. We feared the crossing and would have returned to New Spain if we could have. Then, a narrow flow was found to the north, and the Pimas helped us cross. We exchanged gifts with them, and they gave us fresh food from their gardens.

As we continued northwest across the desert, thick brush scratched our arms and legs, and dust and alkali were tossed at us by icy winds. Our animals suffered, too. Some of them strayed and died. When we finally found water, the animals drank until there was little left. We bundled grass for them and bottled the last of the water. Our leader divided the animals into three herds so they would arrive at the water holes at different times. That way, the water holes would have time to fill again for each herd.

Then the ground froze, and more animals died. At one point, the animals stampeded back to the last water hole. We could not stop them, and many of them froze to death, but, somehow, we survived. On Christmas, we camped near a village of native people. The cold and snow had surprised them, too, so they had nothing that they could offer our animals or us. They did not even have wood for fires.

Without horses for everyone, we could not continue our journey. Our leader sent soldiers on to Mission San Gabriel. They returned with horses, but brought few supplies. As we slowly made our way to the mission, bandits stole some of our animals, and more horses died from the harsh weather. We waited at San Gabriel for supplies from another mission.

Travel to the mission at San Luis Obispo was uneventful. The long, difficult journey had made us despondent, but our spirits improved after we celebrated our safe arrival, and we gave thanks that we would soon be in Monterey. If it had not been for the rain and the mud, we would have reached our destination much sooner.

We expected to find a town and shelter in Monterey, but because the settlement was new, there weren't enough buildings to shelter us. We had to huddle inside our tents during the storms. Even so, we gave thanks that we did not have to endure a longer journey. Some of our party would go farther north to a great bay, but our family stayed in Monterey. We looked for land and began the construction of our adobe house.

A galleon sets sail for New Spain tomorrow. I don't know when it will arrive, but we have given the captain spring water and fresh vegetables for his table in return for delivering this letter. I have been told that the letter will be taken north from the port of Acapulco by mule train, along with other mail and supplies. It may be a year before you receive this message, but it comes with great love from all of our family.

Antonio

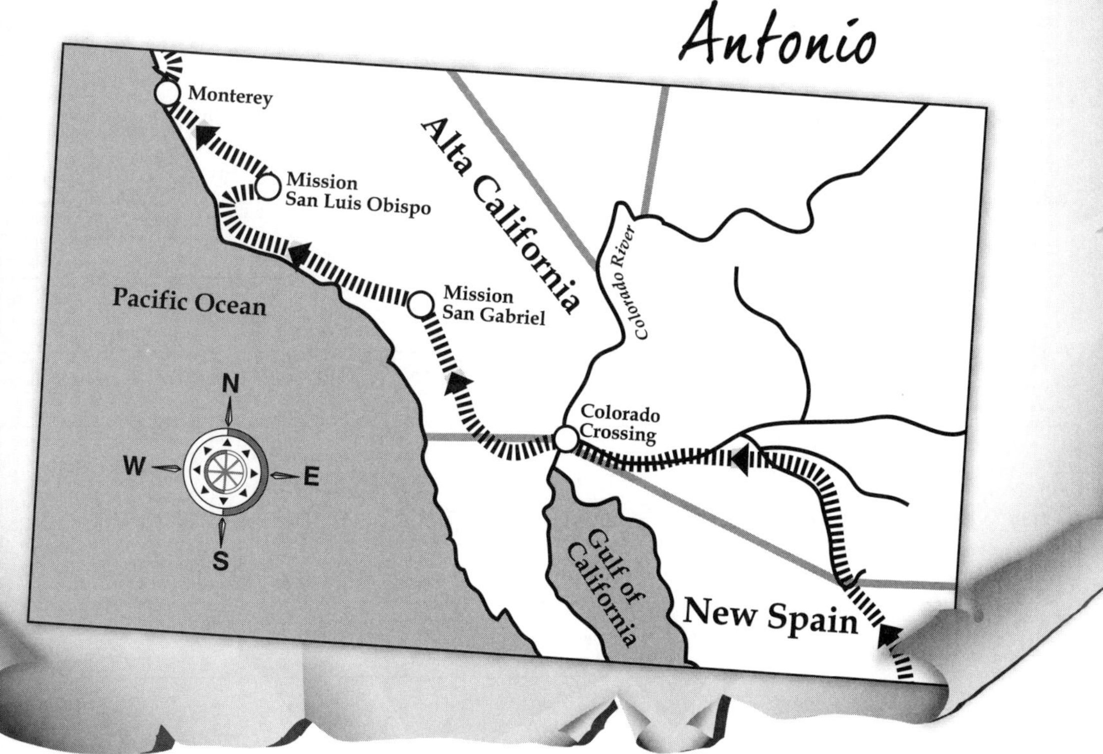

Name ____________________

Questions About *Journey North*

1. In what year did Antonio and his family leave New Spain? ____________

2. Why did Antonio's parents discourage the rest of the family from joining them in Alta California?

3. How was Antonio helping his family?

4. Why do you think that Antonio's parents asked him to write the letter?

5. Was Juan Bautista de Anza a good leader? Explain your answer.

6. List four hardships the caravan faced on the trip to Alta California.

7. Why will it take a long time for Antonio's grandfather to receive the letter?

Name ______________________________

Journey North

Vocabulary

Write the correct word from the list below on the line to complete each sentence.

despondent	galleon	comforts	adobe
hardships	fording	alkali	caravan

1. ______________________ bricks are made of sun-dried clay mixed with straw.
2. In the eighteenth century, a large sailing ship was called a ______________________.
3. A ______________________ is a large group of travelers on a long overland journey.
4. Difficulties that cause sorrow or suffering are ______________________.
5. ______________________ is a mineral salt.
6. When people lose hope and courage, they become ______________________.
7. ______________________ are things that make life easier or more enjoyable.
8. ______________________ a river means wading across at a shallow point.

Pronouns

Read each sentence below. Then review the story and write the noun that the pronoun in bold type replaces.

Example: As **I** write this letter, it is spring in the year 1781. ___Antonio___

1. **We** will never be able to return to New Spain. ______________________
2. **He** cared for those who became ill. ______________________
3. …gave us fresh food from **their** gardens. ______________________
4. We could not stop **them**. ______________________
5. The cold and snow had surprised **them**, too. ______________________
6. **They** returned with horses but brought few supplies. ______________________
7. I don't know when **it** will arrive… ______________________
8. **It** comes with great love from all of our family. ______________________

Name ______________________

Journey North

Action Verbs

Find a form of each action verb below in the story and underline it. Then write a sentence using the verb in a present-day situation to show that you know what the word means. Use clues from the story to help you understand the meaning.

1. accompany: ______________________

2. caution: ______________________

3. endure: ______________________

4. exchange: ______________________

5. huddle: ______________________

6. perish: ______________________

7. stray: ______________________

8. suffer: ______________________

9. survive: ______________________

Name ____________________

Sequencing

Number the events below in the order in which they happened in the story.

_______ We traveled to the mission at San Luis Obispo.

_______ Our leader divided the animals into three herds.

_______ We looked for land and began the construction of our adobe house.

_______ On Christmas, we camped near a village of native people.

_______ We reached the camp of a Pima chief on the banks of the Colorado River.

_______ We expected to find a town and shelter in Monterey, but because the settlement was new, there weren't enough buildings to shelter us.

_______ Traveling continued northwest across the desert, thick brush scratched our arms and legs, and dust and alkali were tossed at us by icy winds.

_______ During the first few days of the trip, everyone was in good spirits, even though our progress was very slow.

Generalizing

1. Write a statement that explains why few people traveled from New Spain to Alta California in the 1700s.

____

____

____

2. Write a statement that tells why people might have braved the hardships to travel from New Spain to Alta California.

____

____

____

City of Mystery

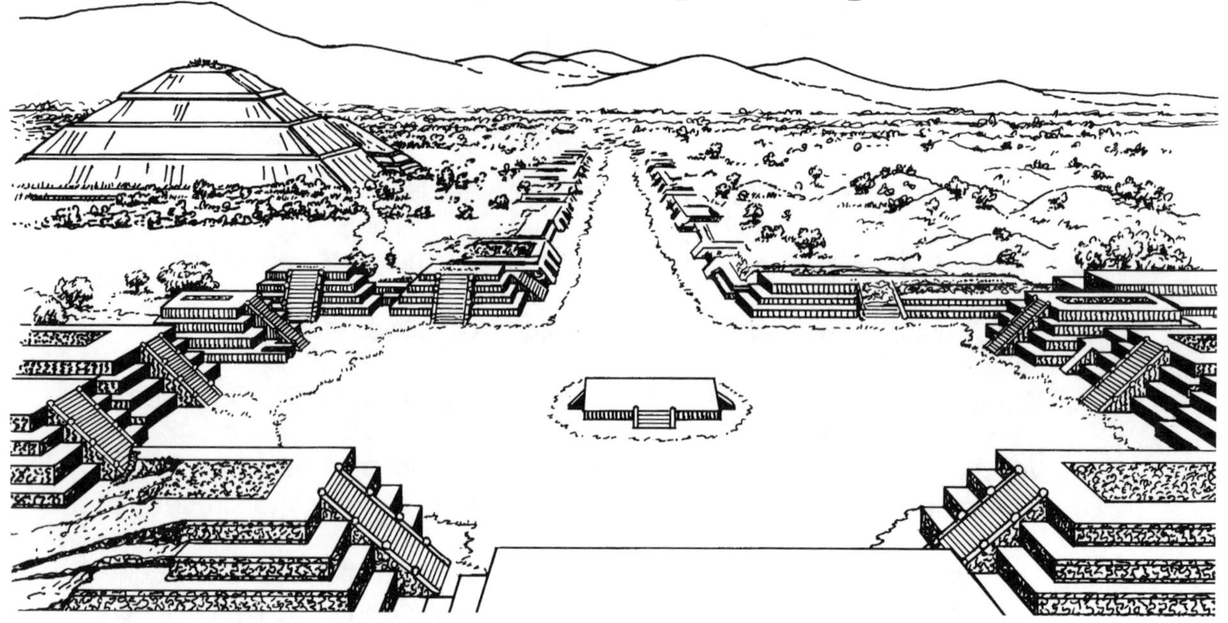

Travelers to central Mexico can visit the ruins of a great city. The ruins can be found about 30 miles (48 kilometers) northeast of Mexico City. No one knows the name of the city or what language its people spoke or who built the city's gigantic pyramids. Scientists have been trying to answer these questions for almost a century.

Every day, archaeologists dig up clues that are helping them learn the facts about this mysterious city. They know that around 100 BC, there were only small villages scattered throughout the area. Three hundred years later, seventy-five thousand people lived in the city. By AD 600, twice as many people lived there. The city had grown to be one of the largest in the world.

The Aztecs, who settled where Mexico City is today, arrived hundreds of years after the ancient city had been destroyed. Discovering the ruins, the Aztecs saw massive apartment complexes, and they marveled at the city's two towering pyramids. They named them the Pyramid of the Sun and the Pyramid of the Moon. The largest, the Pyramid of the Sun, is as tall as a 20-story building! It rises more than 200 feet (61 meters) into the air, and its base covers about 500,000 square feet (46,450 sq m). Because the Aztecs didn't believe that ordinary people could have built such huge structures, they named the ruins *Teotihuacán* (tay-uh-tee-wah-**kahn**), which means "city of the gods."

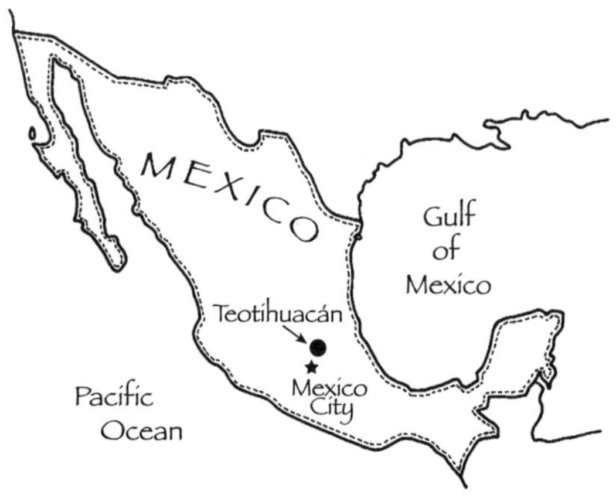

The Aztecs began making pilgrimages to Teotihuacán to pray. They also searched the ruins for artifacts left behind by the people who had lived there. They found pottery and stone masks but nothing made of metal. The knives and other tools they found were made of stone or a type of volcanic rock known as obsidian. No wooden or cloth objects were found because they disintegrate with time.

The walls of some of the city's buildings and underground chambers had huge paintings, or murals, on them. The signs and symbols on the paintings showed that the people of Teotihuacán probably had a system of picture writing. It also seems that the ancient inhabitants of the city studied the stars, the planets, and geometry. Specially marked stones showed that the people measured and used the solar system and the positions of the stars to plan their streets and buildings. The structures were built so that the walls faced north, south, east, and west.

Up to one hundred people probably lived in each of the city's apartment complexes. The living quarters were arranged around a patio. Some of the patios had altars set up on them, at which the residents of the apartments may have left offerings and prayed to their gods. The artifacts found in the apartment areas showed that people came from long distances to live in this city. Perhaps they came because of the marketplace. Some may have been artisans who made objects to trade.

Teotihuacán was a great trading center. Traders came with a variety of goods from faraway places. Chocolate, vanilla, salt, fish, pottery, obsidian, and even elegant bird feathers were probably exchanged in the marketplace. Other valuable trade items included nose plugs and earrings carved from jade, polished obsidian mirrors, and stone images of the feathered serpent god, the storm god, and the great goddess. Jointed pottery dolls and stone masks may also have been offered for sale. While people bargained and exchanged goods in the marketplace, incense burning in large pots by the temples perfumed the air.

Many ceramic figures of people have been unearthed in Teotihuacán. Were their 1,500-year-old faces modeled after ordinary citizens or important officials? That's one of the questions archaeologists and anthropologists are still trying to answer.

Will all the questions about this city of mystery be answered one day? Scientists haven't given up looking for more pieces to this ancient puzzle. If you decide to become an archaeologist and dig up the past, you, too, could help solve the mysteries of Teotihuacán.

Name ____________________

Questions About *City of Mystery*

1. Why is Teotihuacán called the "City of Mystery"?

2. Who named the city *Teotihuacán*? What does the name mean?

3. How tall is the Pyramid of the Sun? How much ground does it cover?

4. Why do you think archaeologists didn't find any metal objects in Teotihuacán?

5. What do you think happened to Teotihuacán and the people who lived there?

6. Would you want to have lived in Teotihuacán? Explain why or why not.

Name ____________________

City of Mystery

Vocabulary

A. Write the number of each word on the line next to the correct meaning.

1. anthropologist	______	to view with wonder or astonishment
2. archaeologist	______	many buildings or units together in a single group
3. complex	______	to discuss an agreeable payment or price
4. artifact	______	the remains of a city that was destroyed
5. obsidian	______	a journey to a religious place
6. disintegrate	______	a dark, glassy rock that is used as a gem
7. bargain	______	an object from an earlier or ancient time
8. pilgrimage	______	a person who studies people and their cultures
9. marvel	______	to fall apart or decay into very small pieces or particles
10. ruins	______	a person who looks for and studies the objects and structures of ancient times

B. Fill in the blank with the correct word from the list below to complete each sentence.

system scattered marketplace ceramic incense murals

1. The great city grew from small villages that were ____________________ around the area.
2. The walls of underground chambers had ____________________ painted on them.
3. The people of Teotihuacán probably used a ____________________ of painted signs and symbols for writing.
4. Traders brought many goods from far away to the ____________________ at Teotihuacán.
5. Burning ____________________ perfumed the air around the temples.
6. Many ____________________ figures and clay masks of people have been found in the ruins.

Name ____________________

Prefixes and Suffixes

Prefixes and **suffixes** are added to base (root) words to change their meanings. Different prefixes and suffixes sometimes change the meanings of words in the same way.

Example: The prefixes **un** and **dis** can both mean *not having* or *without*.

unkindness—*without kindness*
discomfort—*without comfort*

Use the meanings of the following prefixes and suffixes to help you write a definition for each of the words below.

Prefixes: **un, dis** not, not being; not having, without; (to do) the opposite of

Suffixes: **er, ist, ant/ent** a person or thing that does a particular action (makes, works with, studies, knows, plays, specializes in)

1. unearthed: ____________________
2. trader: ____________________
3. inhabitant: ____________________
4. disintegrated: ____________________
5. scientist: ____________________
6. archaeologist: ____________________
7. discover: ____________________
8. traveler: ____________________
9. anthropologist: ____________________
10. resident: ____________________

Name ______________________________

Write About It

Imagine that it is three hundred years in the future. You are an archaeologist, digging at the site where your school is located today. Write a paragraph describing the objects you are finding and explain how the objects show what went on at your school.

Nancy Lopez and Family

It was 1965. Eight-year-old Nancy Lopez was bored following her parents around the golf course. A doctor had told Nancy's mother, Marina, to exercise regularly, so each day, Marina and Nancy's father, Domingo, played golf at Cahoon Park in Roswell, New Mexico, and Nancy had to go along. Finally, she asked her parents if she could play, too. Domingo handed Nancy one of Marina's golf clubs and gave her a few quick pointers. With another group of golfers playing behind them, Domingo had no time to give his daughter a real lesson.

Whack! Whack! Whack! Nancy knocked the ball across the grass, laboring to keep up with her parents and to stay ahead of the other golfers. After that, she played every day. Her father taught her the golf strokes and when to use the various clubs. She practiced with her mother's adult-sized clubs. The clubs were too big for Nancy, but she loved golf, and her game got better and better. Before many months passed, she knew how to send the ball rocketing down the course, high over the heads of her startled parents.

Nancy's parents did all they could to help her game. Realizing that the course at Cahoon Park had no sand traps, Domingo dug a big hole in the family's backyard and filled it with sand. Now Nancy could practice hitting the ball out of a sand trap. Sand traps are large sandy areas on a golf course. Because hitting balls out of the sand is very difficult, sand traps make the game more challenging.

Like most parents, Domingo and Marina Lopez wanted a lot for their daughter Nancy and her older sister, Delma, but golfing was expensive, and the Lopez family didn't have a lot of money. Domingo and Marina worked hard and denied themselves many things so that Nancy could compete in the sport she loved.

Domingo taught Nancy everything he knew about golf. He coached her through problems and cheered her successes. When Nancy was nine, she competed in the state Pee Wee tournament and won! In golf, the lowest score wins, and Nancy's score was so low that she would have won even if she had competed against the older kids in the tournament.

Nancy was eleven when she first outscored her father in a game of golf. It was a close game, but they were both proud of her accomplishment, and years later, Domingo still had her score card from that day displayed in his office. When Nancy was twelve, she amazed everyone by winning the state Women's Amateur tournament, competing against adults, and she then went on to win the U.S. Golf Association's national competition for junior girls—twice!

Nancy Lopez lit up golf courses with her bright smile and her warm, friendly calmness. She made being a champion look easy, but it was not. She worked very hard and faced many barriers. Because the high school she attended had no golf team for girls, she asked to play on the boys' team. The school, however, would not allow it. Disappointed but determined, she asked again, and this time, with an attorney's help, the school allowed her to try out. It was a good decision. With Nancy on the team, the school won the state championship two years in a row.

Nancy and her family had racial prejudices to overcome, too. Some of the competitions Nancy wanted to enter required a country club sponsor. The club in Roswell, however, didn't want the Mexican American Lopez family as members. Fortunately, a country club in Albuquerque did. They were grateful for the chance to make Nancy's family honorary members.

By 1977, everyone knew that Nancy Lopez had a bright future in professional golf. At twenty-one, she "turned pro," which means playing in tournaments to win money, and she wanted to pay back her family for all they had done for her. She especially wanted to buy her mother a new house.

In her first year as a professional golfer, Nancy placed second in several tournaments. Then, tragically, Marina Lopez died. During this hard time for her family, Nancy took some time off from golf. When she came back, she still thought about her mother a lot, and her game was not as effective as she wanted it to be. Her father told her to just let things happen. And things *did* happen.

In 1978, Lopez blew through the world of professional golf like a warm, friendly wind, shattering records and winning five tournaments in a row. She won a total of nine tournaments that year and was named both Rookie of the Year and Player of the Year.

In 1982, the world of golf had to start sharing Lopez with a larger family. In October, she married Ray Knight, a major league baseball player, and between 1983 and 1991, she had three daughters. Although Lopez retired from professional golf after the 2002 season, she has still played occasional tournaments, and her hard work, her calmness, and her smile are still known and admired throughout the world.

Name ______________________________

Questions About *Nancy Lopez and Family*

1. What circumstances caused Nancy Lopez to learn to play golf?

2. How long had Lopez been playing golf before she turned pro?

3. Describe an obstacle Lopez faced as a young female golfer. Then describe an obstacle she faced as a Mexican American.

4. Why do you think that Lopez didn't play golf as well as she wanted to after her mother died?

5. What are two reasons that Nancy Lopez is admired throughout the world?

6. Why do you think the author titled this story *Nancy Lopez and Family*?

Name ______________________________

The Jargon of Golf

Like most sports, golf has its own **jargon**, or special language, that is used to describe the game. Use the golf terms listed below to fill in the blanks in the following paragraphs. The paragraphs contain additional golf terms in bold type.

hole	amateur	course	stroke	tournaments
rookie	sand traps	sponsor	clubs	professional

A game of golf is played on a landscaped outdoor ____________________ that has grass, trees, and plants. It also has **hazards**, such as water holes, hills, and ____________________, where hitting the ball is more difficult, which makes the game more challenging. During a game, a **caddie** helps a golfer by handling the ____________________ that the golfer uses to hit the ball. Golfers use their bodies as well as their arms to **swing** at the golf ball. Each swing the golfer takes is called a ____________________, and the number of swings taken determines the golfer's score. The golfer's goal is to **drive** the ball toward a neatly mowed grassy area, called a **green**, and into a ____________________ marked with a flag. When a golfer hits a ball into the **rough**, an area that is not mowed or landscaped, extra swings may be needed to hit it out, which hurts the golfer's score.

Golfers compete against each other in ____________________. A young golfer who is just starting to compete is an ____________________, who may win a title or a trophy but does not receive any prize money. A ____________________ golfer earns money playing golf and competing. In a golfer's first season playing for money, he or she is called a ____________________. Many golfers depend on companies or organizations to ____________________ them, or pay their expenses for entering competitions. In exchange, golfers often wear clothing that advertises the company.

Name ____________________

Nancy Lopez and Family

Cause and Effect

Complete each sentence below. At the end of the sentence, circle **C** or **E** to indicate whether you wrote a **cause** or an **effect**.

1. Because Nancy was bored following her parents around the golf course, ____________

   ____. C E

2. Nancy's dad built a sand trap in their backyard so that ____________

   ____. C E

3. Nancy's parents made a lot of sacrifices to help her compete because ____________

   ____. C E

4. ____ because

   her high school did not have a golf team for girls. C E

5. Nancy needed help from an attorney because ____________

   ____. C E

6. The country club in Roswell would not accept Mexican Americans as members, so

   ____. C E

7. Because Nancy turned pro, ____________

   ____. C E

8. Nancy was a popular golfer because ____________

   ____. C E

Name ______________________________

Think About It

1. Nancy Lopez has always loved playing golf. What do you love to do? Explain why.

2. Nancy's family helped her become a winning golfer. Write a paragraph that explains how someone helped you achieve a goal.

3. Write about how you have helped someone else. Explain what happened and how helping that person made you feel.

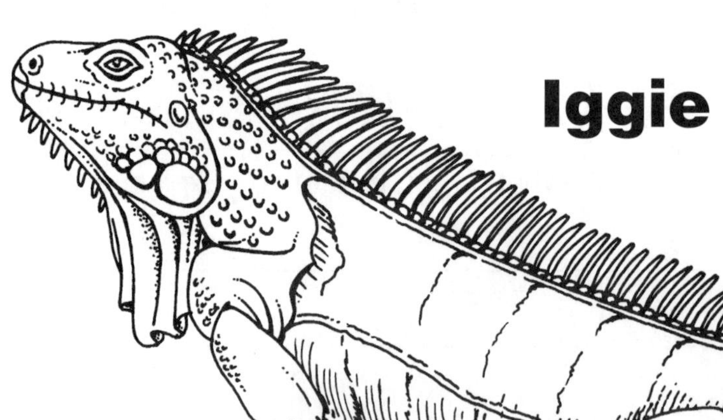

Iggie

Iggie had vanished. That's all there was to it. He had ventured outside before, whenever the window in the kitchen was left open, but Martin had always found him in the garden, sitting in the sun, usually munching on flowers. This time, Iggie didn't seem to be anywhere near the apartment.

Martin lived in an apartment with his Aunt Belle. A year ago, someone had left an iguana in a box in front of the pet store where Aunt Belle worked. She guessed that whoever had owned it left it there because the lizard had grown too big to take care of. But maybe the owner just didn't want it anymore. The pet store didn't have a cage big enough for a full-grown iguana, so Aunt Belle brought it home with her. That was just a week before Martin's birthday. Aunt Belle gave the iguana to Martin as a birthday present. Martin thought that Iggie was the best birthday present he had ever received!

Now Martin was worried. The nights were getting colder, and iguanas need to stay warm. Martin and his friend Arnold searched the garden, looking carefully under every bush and shrub. They knocked on apartment doors and talked to the people who happened to be at home. Mr. Kennon in 3A had seen an iguana outside the laundry room early that morning, so Martin and Arnold searched the laundry room. They looked behind the machines, under the tables, and even inside the washers and dryers.

"Maybe Iggie got locked in someone's apartment by mistake," Arnold said. "We could check it out. He likes to sit in a sunny window."

Martin and Arnold walked around the apartments, looking in each window. The lady who lived in the apartment above Aunt Belle's jerked her blinds shut when she saw what the boys were doing, but in the apartment next to her, Aunt Mary waved enthusiastically and hollered, "Come on in!"

Martin asked Aunt Mary if she had seen Iggie. Aunt Mary wasn't really anyone's aunt; everyone just called her that.

"I've been in and out all day," Aunt Mary answered. "My sister's been sick, so I did some of her laundry to help her out. I drove a big basket of clothes over to her this afternoon, but I didn't see your iguana anywhere. If I had seen that green, scaly creature, I think I would have hollered real loud. You know I'm not much for animals without fur, but I hope you find him soon. Then again, I hope you don't!"

Martin and Arnold searched all around the parking lot, even under the cars. After watching a car zoom into a parking space, Martin said to Arnold, "Iggie would like the warm pavement here, but this sure wouldn't be a good place for an iguana."

"You got that right!" said Arnold. "Iggie would be so scared that he'd lose his tail here for sure." But neither Arnold nor Martin saw a lizard's long tail lying anywhere on the pavement.

"Let's look through the garbage cans," Martin suggested. "Iggie could have smelled something he wanted to eat, and there are always lots of bugs around those cans, too."

Martin and Arnold borrowed some gloves from Angela, one of the maintenance workers. Then they looked in all the garbage cans, holding their noses with one hand and shaking cans with the other. No long tails or spiny backs poked out of the garbage.

Back at the apartment, Martin set a bowl of mealworms and a piece of banana outside the front door.

"Iggie won't eat unless he's warm, but I guess it can't hurt to leave something out for him," Martin told Arnold.

At sunset, Arnold went home for dinner. Martin sat on a tall stool by the kitchen window as he ate the potato soup Aunt Belle had warmed up for him. Every few minutes, he looked outside. He also saw Aunt Belle looking out the window from time to time. "Aunt Belle must be worried, too," he thought.

"You might as well give up for now," Aunt Belle said. "Iggie probably found himself a warm spot for the night."

"A warm spot! That's it!" Martin thought. Iguanas always head for the warmest place around. He and Arnold had looked everywhere warm they could think of—the dryers in the laundry room, under the cars in the parking lot. But now, Martin suddenly remembered what Aunt Mary said about taking the laundry to her sister. A basket of warm laundry, right out of the dryer, was a perfect place for an iguana!

"Aunt Belle!" Martin shouted. "I've got to talk to Aunt Mary right away."

"Her number's by the phone," Aunt Belle told him.

It didn't take long for Martin to convince Aunt Mary that they ought to take a look at the basket of laundry she had taken to her sister. Aunt Mary got permission from Aunt Belle to drive Martin across town to her sister's apartment.

"Now don't get your hopes up, Martin," Aunt Mary said as Martin climbed into her car. "I'm sure I would have noticed an iguana's long tail poking out of the laundry basket if the creature had crawled in there."

Aunt Mary's sister was sitting in a chair watching TV when they arrived.

"Funny joke," she said to Aunt Mary as she pointed to a motionless Iggie stretched out on top of the TV. "Where did you get such a real-looking stuffed toy? I think it looks real cute on top of the TV, don't you?"

Martin and Aunt Mary laughed as they watched Iggie climb down the front of the TV and make his way over to Martin.

Aunt Mary's sister shrieked, "It's got batteries!"

Martin picked up Iggie and set him on his shoulder.

"It's not a toy," Aunt Mary told her sister. "Iggie is Martin's pet. He must have crawled into the laundry basket this morning and hidden under the warm clothes."

"I can't believe I let a *live* lizard sit on my bed," Aunt Mary's sister squealed. "I carried it around the house all afternoon and even showed it to my neighbor."

"Next time you're sick, I'll bring Martin and Iggie for a visit," said Aunt Mary. "You look a lot better now. Iguana-sitting seems to agree with you."

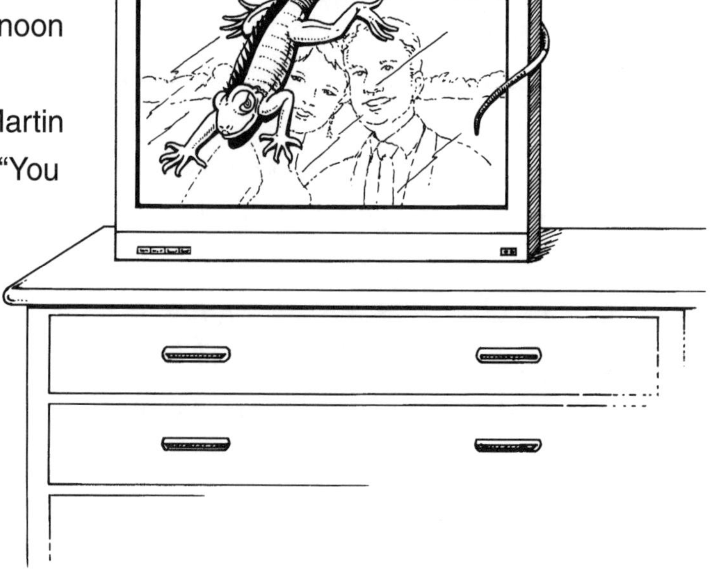

Name ________________________

Questions About *Iggie*

1. How did Martin get a pet iguana?

____

____

____

2. List the places Martin and Arnold looked for Iggie.

   a. ______________________________

   b. ______________________________

   c. ______________________________

   d. ______________________________

   e. ______________________________

3. What made Martin think that Iggie might have hidden in the laundry basket Aunt Mary took to her sister?

____

____

4. Explain why Aunt Mary's sister might have thought that Iggie was a stuffed toy.

____

____

____

5. What kind of person do you think Aunt Mary is? Use facts from the story to support your answer.

____

____

____

Name ______________________

Iggie

Action Verbs Crossword

Match the action verbs in the word box with the definitions below to complete the crossword puzzle.

Word Box	
arrive	search
borrow	set
check	shake
convince	shriek
guess	stretch
head	suggest
holler	vanish
jerk	venture
knock	wave
munch	worry
poke	zoom

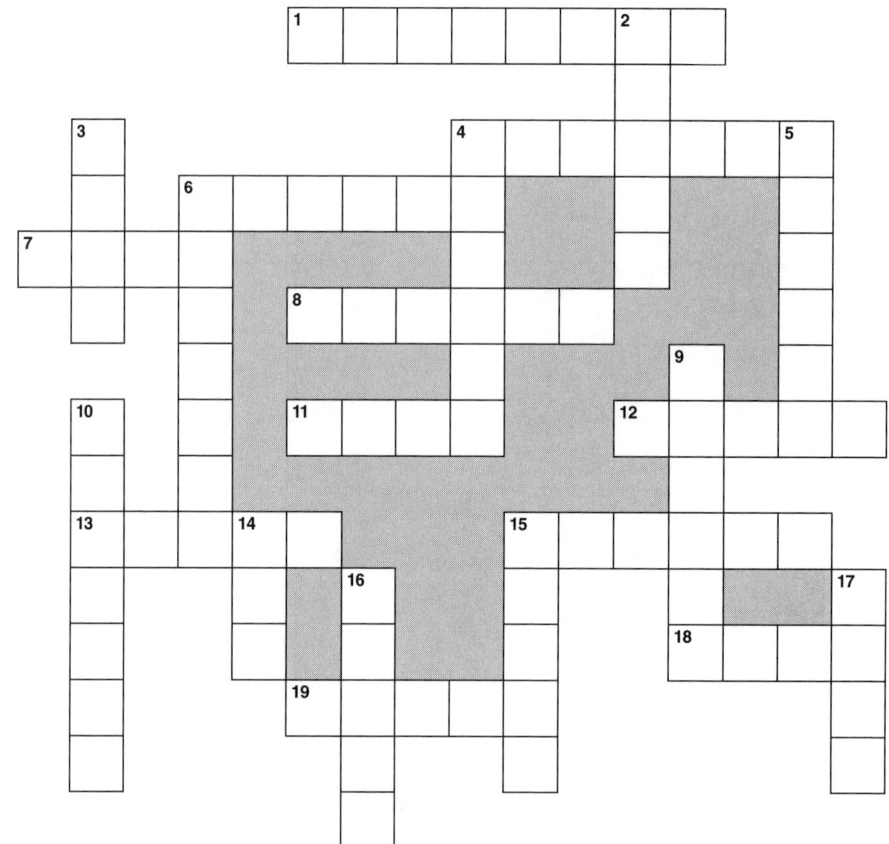

Across

1. to talk someone into doing or believing something; to persuade
4. to pull out or reach for greater length
6. to disappear suddenly
7. to push through
8. to reach a destination
11. to pull with sudden, sharp movements
12. to feel uneasy or concerned about someone or something
13. to state an opinion without being certain of the facts
15. to look for very carefully
18. to move the hand up and down at the wrist
19. to hit or rap with the knuckles

Down

2. to test an idea for accuracy or to look at the condition of something
3. to move quickly with a humming sound
4. to scream with fright
5. to yell or shout
6. to try something risky or dangerous
9. to take as a loan from someone
10. to offer an idea for consideration
14. to put down or place in position
15. to move up and down or back and forth with short, quick motions
16. to chew with crunching sounds
17. to move purposely in a certain direction

Name ______________________

Iggie

Describe Iggie

Fill in the blanks with adjectives from the story that describe Iggie.

1. size ______________
2. with sharp ridges down his back ______________
3. covered with thin plates ______________
4. sitting absolutely still ______________

Nouns to Know

Determine the meaning of the underlined word to help you answer each question.

1. What kind of lizard is Iggie?

____

2. Why did the maintenance worker have gloves to lend to Martin and Arnold?

____

3. Why might Iggie be found sitting on the pavement in the parking lot?

____

4. Why did Aunt Mary's sister shriek, "It's got batteries!"?

____

5. Why did Martin get permission to go with Aunt Mary to her sister's apartment?

____

6. Why would Iggie crawl into a basket of laundry?

____

7. Why did Martin put mealworms in a bowl outside his front door?

____

Name ______________________________

Iggie

Summarizing

Write a headline that summarizes each part of the story. Then write two details that add more information for that part of the story.

Beginning: ______________________________

____

____

____

____

Middle: ______________________________

____

____

____

____

End: ______________________________

____

____

____

____

Justice for All

The Legacy of Martin Luther King, Jr.

On July 2, 1964, the United States Congress passed a Civil Rights Act. It was not the first set of civil rights laws enacted in the United States, but it has been the first law to last. The first Civil Rights Act was passed in 1875, ten years after the end of the American Civil War between the free states of the north (the Union) and the slave states of the south (the Confederacy).

The Civil War ended on April 9, 1865. During the next five years, Congress passed three constitutional amendments in an effort to undo the injustices of the past. The Thirteenth Amendment abolished slavery. The Fourteenth Amendment made former slaves citizens of the United States. The Fifteenth Amendment gave these new citizens the right to vote. The Civil Rights Act passed in 1875 took these amendments one step further by outlawing discrimination in public places. The shameful story of America's mistreatment of African Americans seemed to be in its final chapter.

Unfortunately, in 1883, the U.S. Supreme Court invalidated the Civil Rights Act of 1875. African American citizens could again be legally barred from "white" establishments, and southern states even found ways to get around the Fifteenth Amendment's mandates, threatening the jobs and lives of black citizens who registered to vote.

Nearly one hundred years after the Civil War, Martin Luther King, Jr., stood in the city of Montgomery, Alabama, mourning the lack of progress the nation had made in assuring the civil rights of all citizens. Born in Alabama in 1929 to an African American minister and his wife, King himself endured injustices because of the color of his skin.

Although King's childhood was typical in many ways, he could not go to "white" schools or drink from "white" drinking fountains. White neighbors once asked him to stop playing with their son, and when King was shopping with his mother one day, a white woman struck him on the cheek and called him an offensive name.

1929–1968

On another shopping trip, a shoe salesman refused service to King's father because the senior King, who was also a civil rights leader, would not sit in the "black section" of the store. Martin Luther King, Jr., had cause to be angry, but he did not believe that anger would solve the problems of injustice. He believed the answers could be found in love.

After King finished his schooling, he became the pastor of a church in Montgomery, Alabama. He had enjoyed comfortable freedoms in the northern colleges he had attended. Now he felt called to help African Americans in the South experience those same freedoms. Just how he could change things, however, was not clear. About a year later, he saw a possible path.

On December 1, 1955, an African American woman named Rosa Parks was arrested for refusing to give up her seat on a city bus to a white passenger. Mistreatment of blacks on Montgomery city buses was common. Bus drivers called them hateful names and often drove away from bus stops before black passengers could board. More than once, black citizens were arrested when they refused to offer their seats to white people. But something was different this time. Rosa Parks called the National Association for the Advancement of Colored People (NAACP) to ask for help. Her case would go to court.

News of the Parks case spread quickly in the city of Montgomery, and people gathered at Reverend King's church to form a plan. Montgomery blacks would refuse to ride the bus the following Monday. They would take cars or taxis to work, or they would walk or just stay home. Thousands of fliers were printed and passed out, and the boycott worked! The buses in Montgomery were nearly empty on the morning of December 5, 1955.

Black leaders decided to continue the boycott until African Americans were treated fairly on the buses, and they elected Reverend King president of the group that would oversee the plan. The boycott continued for an entire year. At last, on December 20, 1956, the buses of Montgomery, Alabama, became integrated. Martin Luther King, Jr., was no longer a single individual who felt called to correct injustices. He was now the leader of a massive movement for civil rights.

The Montgomery boycott was just the beginning. Next, King became president of the Southern Christian Leadership Conference. The SCLC was an organization that asked people of all colors and walks of life to break unjust laws. To oppose laws that forced blacks to sit in the backs of buses, Freedom Riders rode buses all over the South, and they would sit anywhere they liked. Sit-ins were held at restaurants and theaters, during which blacks sat in seats reserved for whites. Blacks also conducted kneel-ins at "white" churches.

King next organized marches to show government officials that people were ready to outlaw segregation. Throngs of people joined in these marches. A march on Washington in August 1963 drew a crowd of 250,000. In front of the Lincoln Memorial, many famous people spoke about the need for civil rights. Martin Luther King, Jr., was the day's final speaker. His speech, "I Have a Dream," expressed hope for a day when people of all races would live in harmony. The speech was met with thunderous applause and is still quoted throughout the world today. And the Civil Rights Act passed by Congress in 1964 is still enforced today.

Proving that nonviolent reform is possible, Martin Luther King, Jr., earned the 1964 Nobel Peace Prize. King united hundreds of thousands of people in a struggle for justice. His eloquent speeches, remarkable courage, and insistence on peaceful protests brought people of all races together.

It was not always easy for King to persuade his followers, or even himself, that injustices must be repaid with love. King and his family received hundreds of threatening phone calls. His house, his brother's house, and fellow pastors' houses were bombed. Many churches were bombed, too. Southern states used old laws to arrest thousands of protesters. Marchers were attacked by police dogs and blasted with water from fire hoses. People were injured, and people were killed. Some black leaders wanted to fight violence with violence, but King stood behind his belief in the power of love.

Sadly, on April 4, 1968, Reverend King was killed by a sniper's bullet. The man who refused to turn to anger, hate, or violence was killed by violence at the age of 39. Still, his dream lives on as the entire world continues working toward the day when all people, regardless of color, can live in peace and enjoy civil justice. Martin Luther King, Jr., can be thanked for defining the dream.

Name ______________________

Questions About *Justice for All*

1. What kind of discrimination did Martin Luther King, Jr., experience as a boy?

2. How did Rosa Parks influence Reverend King?

3. What was unique about Reverend King's approach to creating justice for all?

4. Why do you think that marches were effective ways to promote civil rights reform?

5. What possible connection might there have been between the March on Washington in 1963 and the Civil Rights Act of 1964?

6. What do you think were Martin Luther King, Jr.'s, greatest challenges?

Name ______________________________

Vocabulary

A. Write an example from the story on the lines after each word below to show that you understand the meaning of the word. On the line in front of each word, write **P** if the word relates to a problem or **S** if it relates to a solution.

Example: __P__ discrimination: Black children were not allowed to attend the same schools as white children.

1. ______ injustice: ______________________________
2. ______ sit-ins: ______________________________
3. ______ mistreatment: ______________________________
4. ______ boycotts: ______________________________
5. ______ integration: ______________________________

B. Write the letter of the correct definition on the line in front of each phrase or term.

______ invalidate a law	a. the freedoms given to citizens
______ endure injustices	b. making changes through peaceful means
______ legally bar	c. to make or pass a law
______ civil rights	d. to use the law to prevent the exercise of rights
______ enact a law	e. a warning of intention to cause harm
______ nonviolent reform	f. to claim that the law no longer has to be obeyed
______ a threatening action	g. objecting in a nonviolent way
______ peaceful protests	h. to tolerate unfair treatment or discrimination

Name ____________________

Think About It

A. A **legacy** is something that is passed on from one generation to another. Write a paragraph describing Martin Luther King's legacy to the people of America.

B. Think about an unfair situation that made you very angry. Describe the problem and then compare how you handled it with how Martin Luther King, Jr., might have handled it.

Name ______________________________

Character Map

Add details from the story to complete the character map below. Write two details in each box to describe that characteristic of Martin Luther King, Jr.

Brave

1.

2.

Influential

1.

2.

Martin Luther King, Jr.

Peace-Loving

1.

2.

Unselfish

1.

2.

Animal Skyscrapers

Giraffes are big animals. They weigh between 1,800 and 3,000 pounds (816 and 1,360 kilograms) and are the tallest living land animals in the world. The average height of female giraffes is 14 to 16 feet (4.25 to 5 meters). Males average 16 to 18 feet (5 to 5.5 m). At those heights, you could say that giraffes are the skyscrapers of the animal world.

The legs of a giraffe are twice as long as its body. The front legs are longer than the hind legs, making the back of the giraffe slope downward from its shoulders. With such extraordinary legs, giraffes can walk up to 10 miles (16 kilometers) an hour. When a giraffe is in a hurry, it can gallop up to 35 miles (56 km) an hour. As the giraffe walks or runs, its head and neck shift forward and back, helping the tall animal stay balanced and move more quickly.

A giraffe's neck has a lot to do with its height. The necks of these peaceful giants are 6 to 8 feet (2 to 2.5 m) long. A special joint connecting the head and neck allows the giraffe to hold them in a straight line. Pointing straight up, the head adds about 2 feet (61 centimeters) to the giraffe's height. Although a giraffe's neck is longer than any other animal's, it has only seven vertebrae, or neck bones, which is the same number of vertebrae that humans have in their necks.

To pump blood all the way up its long neck to its brain, a giraffe's heart has to work very hard. That hardworking heart is about 2 feet (61 cm) long and weighs about 24 pounds (11 kg). Blood vessels in the brain and special valves in the arteries of the neck control the flow of blood so it doesn't rush to the giraffe's head when the animal lowers its neck.

Giraffes are known to have very good eyesight. They can see something moving over a mile (km) away. Other grazing animals come to a watering place when giraffes are drinking because they know that their tall neighbors can spot trouble coming a long way off. Sometimes, one giraffe keeps watch while the others lower their heads to drink.

Giraffes, like cattle, are ruminants. A ruminant is a cud-chewing animal with a stomach that has four sections. When giraffes eat, they first swallow their food whole. Then they bring undigested food back up to chew it and swallow it again. The food is digested when it reaches the fourth section of the stomach.

Acacia leaves are a giraffe's favorite food. Because these leaves are about three-quarters water, they also provide moisture when there are no watering places nearby. A giraffe's height makes it easy to reach the tops of acacia trees and pull off the tender leaves. The sharp thorns that surround acacia leaves don't bother giraffes. A giraffe can reach around the thorns with its very long tongue. Any thorns the giraffe might accidentally swallow will be coated with thick, sticky saliva from the giraffe's mouth.

The tongue of a giraffe is about 18 inches (46 cm) long. The giraffe uses its tongue not only for eating, but also to keep clean. Giraffes do not bathe. They lick their bodies clean. A giraffe even cleans its nose and ears with its long tongue! Oxpecker birds usually help giraffes with their grooming. The birds walk up and down a giraffe's back, eating insects and getting rid of dry skin and loose hair.

Giraffes' bodies have spotted coats. Each species has its own unique color and pattern of spots. Colors range from yellowish red to dark brown on a cream or tan background. Some giraffes have large, straight-edged spots that are close together. Others have irregular spots with either jagged or rounded edges.

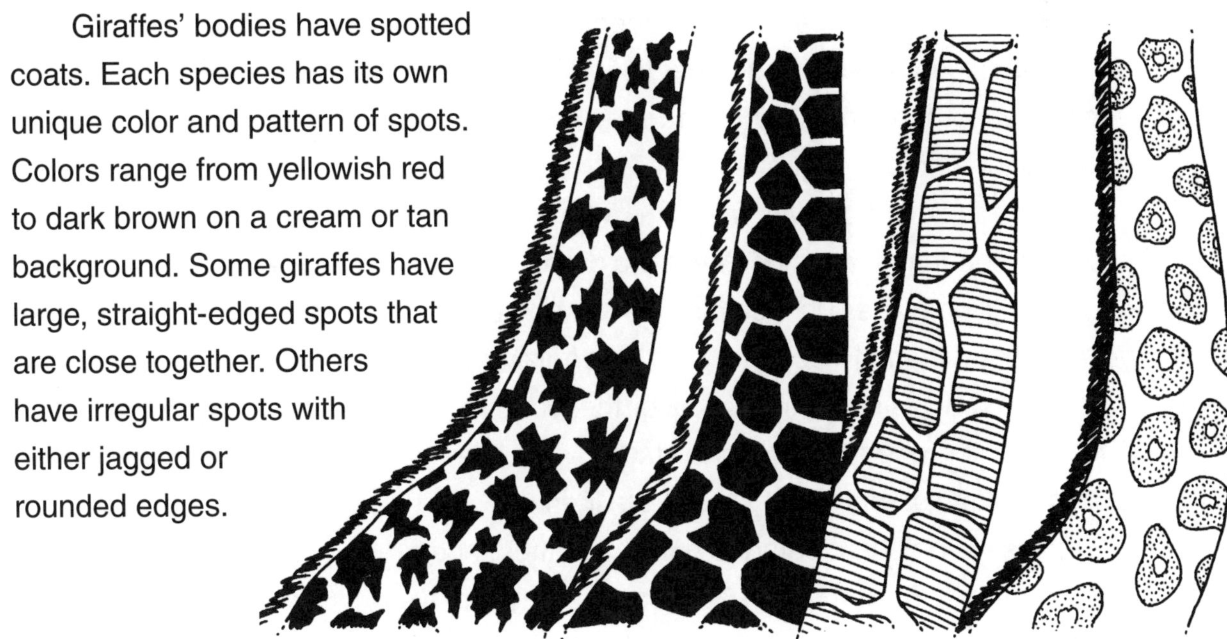

A female giraffe usually has only one baby at a time, and the baby, or calf, is born tall! The height of a newborn calf is about 6.5 feet (2 m), and its neck is very long compared to its body. A mother giraffe guards her calf carefully to protect it from attacks by leopards, lions, hyenas, and wild dogs. Not many of these animals will attack a young giraffe with its mother nearby. If a mother giraffe strikes an attacker with her strong hooves, she can injure the animal so badly that it is no longer able to harm her baby.

Before a mother giraffe goes off to eat, she hides her newborn in tall grass to protect it. After the calf is about a month old, however, all of the young giraffes in a herd are left together in a sheltered area while their mothers search for food. The young giraffes gallop around and play games with each other while they're waiting for their mothers to return. Sometimes, a "baby-sitter" stays with them.

Today, giraffes face a number of threats. With the human population growing in central Africa, where most giraffes are found, people are taking over more and more of the land that giraffes have been living on. Those people also need food, and giraffes can provide large quantities of meat. Already, too many giraffes have been killed for their meat, hides, and tail hair. Droughts and diseases have also reduced the number of giraffes.

Some factors, however, favor the future of giraffes. Farmers and ranchers have learned that giraffes don't eat the crops people grow or the same grasses cattle eat. Sometimes, in fact, giraffes are seen eating tree leaves while the cattle graze around them. People are also recognizing the value of giraffes to Africa's economy. Tourists come from all over the world to see these amazing animals. Their need for food and places to stay creates jobs for the local citizens, and the money tourists spend helps African businesses.

Laws have been created to protect giraffes, and areas of land have been set aside for them. But if these gentle giants are to survive outside of zoos, people must find even more ways to protect them and to preserve their habitats.

Questions About *Animal Skyscrapers*

1. What characteristics do giraffes have that help to protect them?

2. List four facts from the story that contain specific measurements.

3. Why do other animals come to a watering place where they see giraffes drinking?

4. How do oxpeckers help giraffes? How do the giraffes help the oxpeckers?

5. How does the growing human population in central Africa affect giraffes?

6. How are tourists helping to save giraffes?

Name ______________________

Animal Skyscrapers

Vocabulary

A. Write each word listed below on the line next to its definition.

digest	arteries	ruminants	droughts	joint	unique
irregular	shift	preserve	cud	valves	sheltered

1. covered or hidden for protection ______________
2. long periods of time without much or any rain ______________
3. to change positions ______________
4. very unusual; one of a kind ______________
5. cud-chewing animals with four-chamber stomachs ______________
6. not having a uniform shape, size, or pattern ______________
7. swallowed food brought back up for chewing ______________
8. a place where two bones come together ______________
9. to break down food so it can nourish the body ______________
10. to keep from being damaged or destroyed ______________
11. devices that control the flow of fluids in a pipe or a tube ______________
12. tubes that carry blood from the heart to all other parts of the body ______________

B. Find the correct word in the story to answer each question below.

1. What noun describes people who travel far away from home to visit different places? ______________
2. What verb describes the way many large, four-footed animals run? ______________
3. What noun describes people who raise cattle and other grazing animals? ______________
4. What term is used as a synonym for *liquid*? ______________

Name ________________________

Prepositions

A **preposition** is a word at the beginning of a phrase that shows the relationship of a noun or a pronoun to another word in the same sentence. A phrase that begins with a preposition is called a **prepositional phrase**.

Example: Kai needed a box **for** her mother's gift.

The word *for* is a **preposition**. It begins the **prepositional phrase** *for her mother's gift*, which shows the relationship between the words *box* and *gift*.

The words listed below are some common prepositions.

about	at	between	from	off	to
above	before	by	in	on	under
across	behind	down	into	onto	until
after	below	during	near	over	with
around	beneath	for	of	through	without

A. Underline the prepositional phrase in each sentence below.

1. A giraffe is a big animal with a long neck.
2. A special joint connects a giraffe's head to its neck.
3. Giraffes can reach the top leaves of acacia trees.
4. A giraffe brings swallowed food back up into its mouth to chew it.
5. Tourists from many countries visit Africa to see giraffes.

B. Find five phrases in the story that each begin with a different preposition. Write the phrases on the lines below and circle the preposition in each phrase.

1. ________________________
2. ________________________
3. ________________________
4. ________________________
5. ________________________

Name ________________________

Topic Sentences and Supporting Details

Each of the sentences in the outline below states the main topic of a paragraph in the story. Find each paragraph. Then list supporting details from the paragraph on the lines under the topic sentence. Use as few words as possible. You do not have to write complete sentences.

I. Giraffes have good eyesight.

A. ________________________

B. ________________________

II. Each kind of giraffe has a unique pattern of spots.

A. ________________________

B. ________________________

C. ________________________

D. ________________________

III. Giraffes, like cattle, are ruminants.

A. ________________________

B. ________________________

C. ________________________

D. ________________________

Read the supporting details and write a topic sentence on the line.

IV. ________________________

A. licks its body clean

B. can clean its ears and nose with its long tongue

C. Oxpeckers help with grooming.

Two Sisters

A Folk Tale

Not so long ago, two sisters inherited land from their father. The younger sister, Etta, received land that was hilly, dry, and rocky. The older sister, Gretta, was given land planted with fields and orchards. There was even a stream nearby so she could easily water her plants and trees.

Etta didn't complain about her rough land. It was a gift, and she was grateful to have it. She set to work removing rocks, terracing the hills, and cultivating the soil. The work was hard, and she had to walk to the river for water when there wasn't enough rain. Within a few years, however, her land was producing twice as many crops as her sister's fields and orchards.

Gretta harvested her crops, but she never bothered to prepare the soil for the next planting. Soon, her fields grew more weeds than crops. She gathered fruit from the trees in her orchard, but she never took the time to prune the trees. Each year, they had fewer blossoms and produced less fruit. Gretta had no time for her land. She was too busy with meetings and other activities in town. Gretta liked to feel important.

One year, as she watched her sister unload cartloads of produce, Gretta wondered why she had so much less to take to market than Etta. She could not understand how Etta managed so well with land that had never grown anything before. Wanting to know her sister's secret, Gretta started spying on Etta and overheard her talking to a little pear tree.

"Soon, dear tree," said Etta, "you will grow tall and strong, and your magic blossoms will turn to fruit. Then I will take your juicy pears to the marketplace for everyone to admire."

Gretta confronted her sister. "It's magic!" she cried. "I knew it! It would be impossible to grow fruit or vegetables on your worthless land without magic. I will tell everyone that your produce is enchanted."

"It is enchanting perhaps, dear sister, but not enchanted," Etta replied.

"Do you deny that you are using magic to grow your plants and trees?" Gretta demanded.

"I cannot deny that it is magical to see plants and trees grow," Etta answered.

That night, Gretta went back to Etta's orchard and dug up the little pear tree. The next day, she planted it in her own orchard.

"Now I have the magic tree," she said. "Its juicy pears will grow for me, and my sister will have none at all."

When Etta saw that the tree was missing, she guessed what had happened to it. She was sad to lose the tree, but she reasoned that if her sister learned to care for it, Gretta's orchard would be prosperous again. Gretta, however, did not take care of the little tree. She didn't water it. She didn't prune it. She had no time for the little tree, so it soon died, just as her other trees had.

Gretta became very angry. "I don't know my sister's magic words," she said to her cat. "I should have listened more carefully. I must go back and find out."

Etta was watering her apple trees when Gretta sneaked into the orchard. Gretta hid behind a tree, unaware that Etta could see her purple shoes and flowered hat poking out.

"Dear tree," Etta said loudly enough for Gretta to hear, "you rewarded me with sweet fruit this year. So that your magic will continue, I will give you water when your roots are dry and trim your branches when your leaves cloak the ground. Then you can work more magic and fill my baskets with sweet fruit again."

Gretta waited until dark. Then, in the moonlight, she dug up the apple tree and dragged it back to her own orchard. She planted the tree in a large hole and watered it faithfully. When the air was cold and the tree's golden leaves cloaked the ground, she carefully trimmed the branches.

The next spring, the tree was covered with blossoms. Gretta continued to water and care for the tree. Soon, it was covered with apples. Gretta proudly took baskets of the fruit to the marketplace.

One afternoon, Etta came to Gretta's house with a cartload of young trees.

"Dear sister," she said, "now that you know my secret, I have come to help you replant your orchard."

"I just happened to hear your magic words," said Gretta, "so I said them to my apple tree every day, and the tree grew baskets and baskets of fruit."

"Magic words?" Etta asked. "I don't use magic words. My magic comes from two strong branches and from sturdy roots that are not planted in the ground. Perhaps you discovered my real magic without realizing it."

"Nonsense!" Gretta said. "If I had seen any magic branches or roots in your orchard, I would have brought them home with me. Then I would not have had to work so hard."

"If you didn't see them," said Etta, "then you weren't looking in the right place. Watch now. I will put those branches and roots to work once again."

Etta began to dig holes and plant the young trees. When she finished, she hugged her sister and said, "My arms, you see, are the two strong branches, and my legs are the sturdy roots. I create my own magic, Gretta. You have the same roots and branches. If you use them well, you don't need magic words."

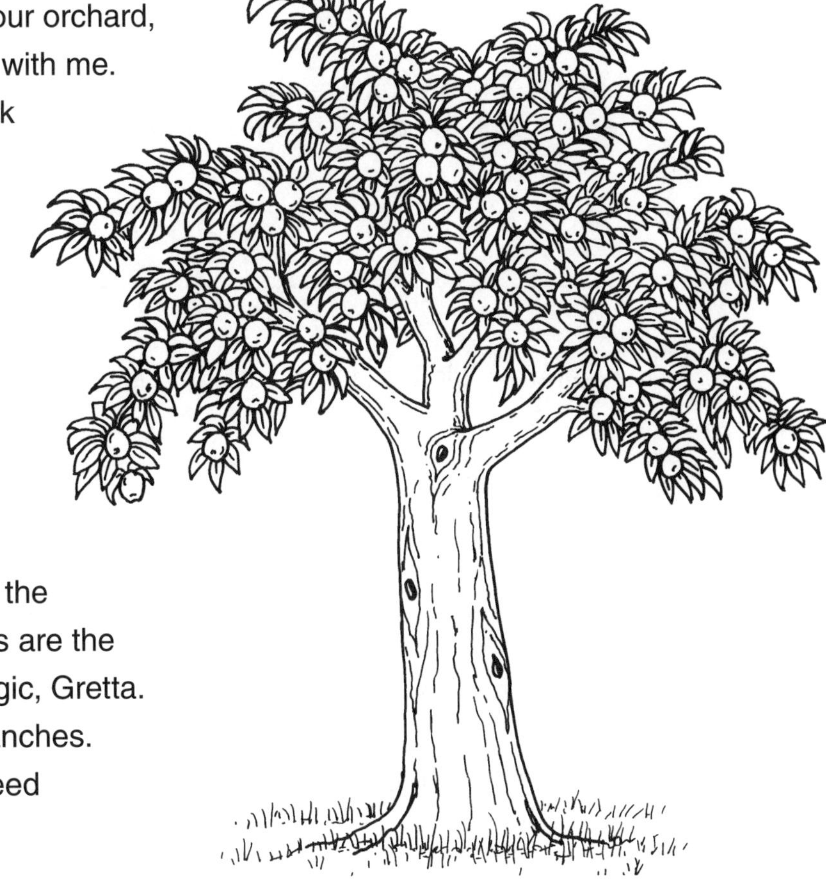

Name ____________________

Questions About *Two Sisters*

1. How was the land that Etta inherited different from the land that Gretta received?

2. What did Etta do to make her land productive?

3. What did Gretta think Etta was doing to get cartloads of fruit and vegetables?

4. What did Gretta think was the reason she was growing so much more fruit after she took the apple tree from Etta's orchard?

5. In what ways did Etta try to help her sister?

6. Explain what Etta meant when she said, "It is enchanting perhaps, dear sister, but not enchanted."

Name ______________________

Two Sisters

Vocabulary

A. Write each word listed below on the line next to its definition.

worthless	enchanted	orchards	complain	inherited
terracing	prosperous	confronted	sturdy	cultivating

1. ______________ strong and steady
2. ______________ under a magic spell
3. ______________ received from someone who has died
4. ______________ making steplike tiers of earth on a sloping hillside
5. ______________ preparing land for planting crops
6. ______________ met face to face to challenge or accuse
7. ______________ without value
8. ______________ fields of trees that produce fruit
9. ______________ successful and productive
10. ______________ to express unhappiness about something that seems wrong or unfair

B. Find words in the story to complete each list below.

words that refer to plants	**words that refer to farm work**
______________	______________
______________	______________
______________	______________
______________	______________
______________	______________
______________	______________

Name ______________________

Two Sisters

Homographs

Homographs are words that are spelled the same and sound the same but have different meanings.

Example: **long**—describing a great distance or amount of time
long—to want very much

Find each word below in the story and underline it. Then fill in the circle next to the meaning of the word as it is used in the story.

1. land
   Ⓐ a large section of ground
   Ⓑ to bring down from the air to the ground
2. crops
   Ⓐ plants grown in large quantities to supply food for people or animals
   Ⓑ removes from around the edges, usually by cutting
3. fields
   Ⓐ catches something (as a baseball) thrown or hit out into the open
   Ⓑ large areas of land used for growing crops
4. roots
   Ⓐ the parts of a plant that grow underground and hold the plant in place
   Ⓑ digs around in the dirt
5. cloak
   Ⓐ a loose-fitting, capelike garment
   Ⓑ to cover or hide from view
6. trim
   Ⓐ a decorative material or design along the border or edge of something
   Ⓑ to clip or cut off a small amount
7. prune
   Ⓐ to trim off or cut away excess or unwanted parts
   Ⓑ a dried plum
8. rocks
   Ⓐ moves back and forth
   Ⓑ large stones
9. leaves
   Ⓐ goes away from a place; departs
   Ⓑ the flat green parts of plants that are attached to the stem
10. stream
   Ⓐ a narrow flow of water
   Ⓑ to flow into or out of
11. watch
   Ⓐ a device for telling time that can be easily worn or carried
   Ⓑ to look at or observe attentively
12. branches
   Ⓐ the limbs of a tree
   Ⓑ separates and goes off in other directions

Name ______________________________

Compare the Characters

Think about the behaviors and personalities of Etta and Gretta. How are the two sisters alike? How are they different? Write at least four words or phrases in each section of the Venn diagram to compare the two characters.

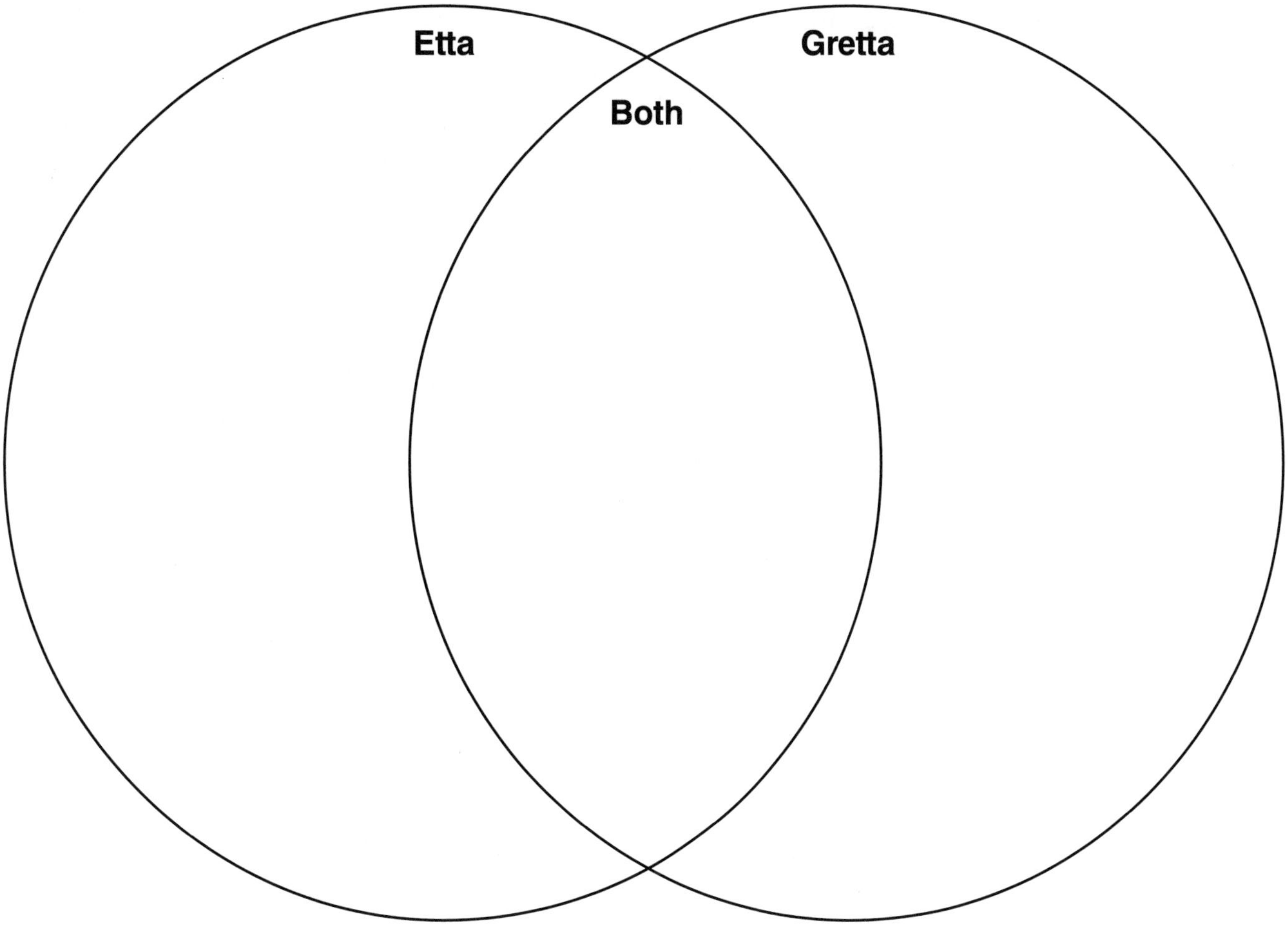

Etta

Both

Gretta

Indiana Sundays

As a child, I loved Sunday afternoons in summer. Precisely at twelve o'clock noon, church let out with the loud ringing of the huge bell. In a flash, my cousins and I burst out the nearest door and climbed into each other's cars in a wild and disorderly fashion. We were off to Grandma and Grandpa's farmhouse!

The first order of business was to devour a large and long noontime dinner. Then we slammed our way outside through Grandma's back door. The fun was about to begin. We chased barn cats, stomped in cow pies, and threw each other into haystacks. We explored every nook and cranny of Grandpa's old barn. Our newest-addition cousins sat in a playpen not far from the volleyball net where the adults gathered. Sometimes, we snatched up the little tykes to take them for rides in wheelbarrows or into the barn to kiss the cows. And young cousins always learned the rules for kick-the-can and king-of-the-hill even before they could speak.

On lucky Sunday afternoons, Grandpa would join us in the field behind the barn. We took turns riding on the old John Deere all around the farm. The cows mooed their complaints when we entered their domain. We just laughed and reached out to pet them on the nose. Sometimes, we even did real work—planting seeds or gathering eggs. The chickens hated Sundays almost as much as the cows did. Grandpa always assured them that we were good and gentle helpers.

Eventually, the sun started to set. The adults stopped their volleyball game, groaning about bug bites, sore muscles, and hunger. Adults and kids alike clamored into the mosquito-free house for supper, which was a makeshift affair, featuring noontime leftovers. After supper, the adults retired to the living room, collapsing onto couches and into rocking chairs. We kids headed for the cellar to battle with cue-stick swords between games of eight ball.

I stayed upstairs sometimes. I silently found a corner on the floor of the adult world and listened. The conversation was always about ethics. Is it ever okay to lie? Do all people have a conscience? Never resolved, the issues were sooner or later shelved for further discussion. The men then moved their party to the cellar. When the door squeaked open at the top of the stairs, the kids left the pool table. It was the grown-ups' turn to play.

For a while, then, we kids explored the basement. There were flowers drying in the cramped quarters behind the massive furnace. There was a tall, rickety old metal box that Grandpa showered in after his shifts on the B&O railroad. There was a fruit cellar full of fresh-fruit bins, and the vegetables that Grandma had canned last fall filled the tall shelves. Eventually, one of us was caught forgetting to shut the fruit cellar door. Besides, we were making too much noise and kept bumping into cue sticks at crucial moments, so we would all be booted upstairs, where the womenfolk offered us a choice. We could play outdoors or move into the "porch." The porch was actually a huge, fully enclosed room. In any self-respecting California ranch home, it would have been called the "recreation room."

Deciding our next move always turned into a debate for us kids. Catching fireflies and moonlight tag were the main outdoor attractions. Games involving the hundreds of buttons from Grandma's button box were an indoor option. Because we usually decided on some mix of indoor and outdoor fun, the porch door slammed frequently, letting bugs into the house. The adults were quick to comment on both annoyances.

Slowly, a few at a time, aunts and uncles surrendered to the threat of another Monday morning arriving too soon. Cousins were coaxed into cars with bribes of Grandma Ruth's cookies. Children's games fell apart, and adult talk slowed with each disappearing brood. My family was always the last to leave, and I was the most reluctant to say goodbye to another Indiana Sunday.

Name ___________________________

Questions About *Indiana Sundays*

1. What is the author's purpose for writing this personal narrative?
   Ⓐ to explain the advantages of a big family
   Ⓑ to persuade readers to live in the country
   Ⓒ to entertain readers with a story about a childhood experience
   Ⓓ to tell readers how to plan large family gatherings

2. Name three of the kids' activities after the noon meal that showed they had no adult supervision.

3. Why do you think that the cows and the chickens "hated Sundays"?

4. What detail in the story shows that the author was interested in the grown-ups' activities?

5. Quote lines from the beginning and the end of the story that express how the author felt about Indiana Sundays.

6. Would you have preferred to explore the barn or the basement? Explain your choice.

Name ______________________________

Vocabulary

Write the number of the correct definition on the line next to each word.

______ makeshift	1. extremely important
______ tykes	2. standards of right and wrong
______ ethics	3. built for temporary use out of available resources
______ conscience	4. made loud noises
______ reluctant	5. an inner sense of right and wrong
______ coaxed	6. offers of money or gifts to get something in return
______ annoyances	7. close to breaking or falling apart; flimsy
______ bribes	8. gently persuaded
______ clamored	9. territory or space
______ crucial	10. hesitant, uncertain, or unwilling
______ rickety	11. small children
______ domain	12. bothersome actions; nuisances

Dialect

A **dialect** is the word usage and pronunciations typical of a certain area or region. This story uses a somewhat old-fashioned dialect that is typical of Indiana and several other midwestern states.

Draw lines to match the words from the story's midwestern dialect with their synonyms.

dinner •	• family
porch •	• basement
cellar •	• lunch
brood •	• corner or small space
womenfolk •	• recreation room
nook and cranny •	• women

Name ______________________________

Idioms

An idiom is a phrase that does not mean exactly what the words say.

Example: *Children's games fell apart* means that the children gradually stopped playing their games.

Find the underlined phrases below in the story and explain what they mean.

1. ...the issues were sooner or later shelved for further discussion.

____

2. ...we would all be booted upstairs...

____

3. ...aunts and uncles surrendered to the threat of another Monday morning arriving too soon.

____

____

Imagery

Imagery is the use of colorful and expressive words and phrases to help readers picture or imagine what the writer is seeing, hearing, smelling, tasting, or feeling.

Example: *We slammed our way outside through Grandma's back door* creates an image, or picture, of the back door slamming behind the children as they raced outside to play.

1. Write four more examples of imagery from the story.

____

____

____

____

2. What piece of farm equipment do you think is described as "old John Deere"?

____

Name ______________________

Read the Map

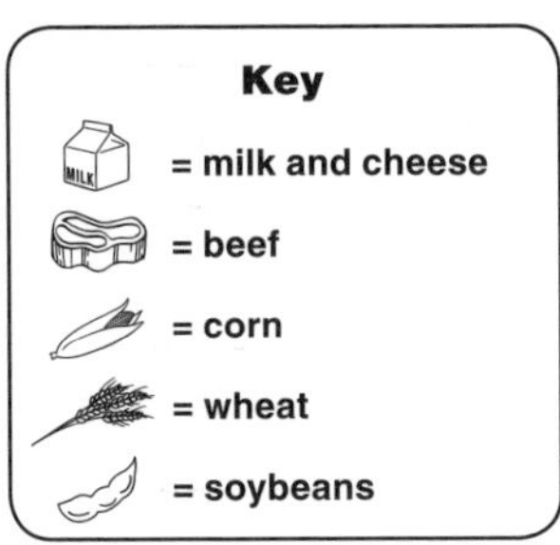

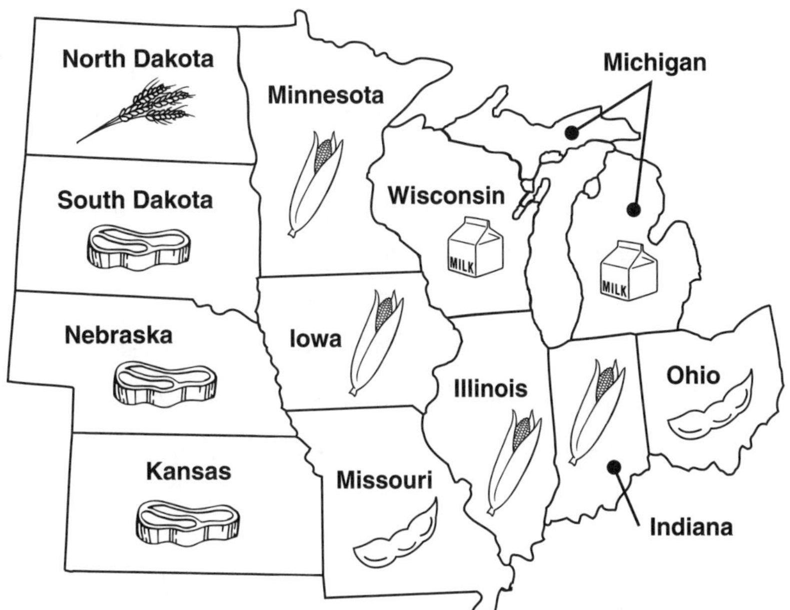

Look at the map and the key above to answer the following questions about the main crops and livestock raised on farms in the midwestern states.

1. What is the main crop grown in the state where the story takes place?

   ____

2. Which states produce what you need to make a bowl of cereal for breakfast?

   ____

3. From which state could factories that make flour buy their grain?

   ____

4. Which states' main product is something that vegetarians do not eat?

   ____

5. Which states would be great places for grilled cheese sandwich lovers to live?

   ____

6. Which states produce legumes?

   ____

America's First Lady of Courage

In the year 1890, the town of Tuscumbia, Alabama, had a law about dogs. Any dog that was found wandering around town without its owner would be put to death. A dog named Lioness roamed the streets of Tuscumbia alone one night. After Lioness was killed, people from all over the United States and Europe sent money to the famous ten-year-old girl who had owned Lioness so the girl could buy a new dog. The girl, however, had other plans for the money. She thanked people for their concern and then asked to use the money to send Tommy Stringer, a poor blind boy, to a special school. At the age of ten, Helen Keller's lifelong career of giving had already begun.

Three years earlier, Helen would not have been able to offer this help. The seven-year-old was trapped inside a dark and quiet world. A fever she had as an infant had left her blind and deaf. She used simple signs to let her family know her needs, but she did not understand language. She did not know that the people around her moved their lips. She did not know that things had names. The trouble she had communicating frustrated Helen. In anger, she threw fragile objects across the room, had wild temper tantrums, and even locked her mother in the pantry.

Helen's parents knew they had to do something about her wild behavior. They hired Annie Sullivan to tutor Helen, and Annie quickly found that she had a challenge on her hands. First, she "tamed" Helen by not giving in to her tantrums. Then, she taught Helen about language. Annie traced patterns on the palm of Helen's hand with her finger. At first, Helen didn't understand that the patterns stood for words. When she began to understand, however, there was no stopping her. She learned so quickly that she became famous worldwide for her accomplishments. She mastered not only English, but also French, German, Greek, and Latin. She later wrote that language freed her, and Helen would spend the rest of her life freeing others with her words.

Annie stayed with Helen for fifty years. When Helen was young, Annie took her on picnics, long walks, and toboggan rides.

She spelled in Helen's hand and translated countless books into Braille for Helen to read. By 1905, Helen had graduated from college with honors, written a book about her life, and learned to speak. After graduation, Helen became a member of the Massachusetts Commission for the Blind.

1880–1968

Then, Helen and Annie hit the road. They were invited to Washington, D.C.; Europe; and Japan. At each stop, they shook hands with presidents, kings, princes, and prime ministers. Most importantly, they spoke to crowds of people. Helen gave other disabled people hope by speaking about the independence she now experienced. Sometimes, she spoke about the unfair treatment of women, the poor, and others who struggled for justice. Helen always asked her audiences to treat themselves and all other people with dignity and respect.

After Annie Sullivan died in 1936, Helen missed her dearly. She started writing a book about Annie. When her notes for the book were destroyed in a house fire, she began a new book, and in 1955, *Teacher* was published.

Helen lived another 32 years after Annie died. With the help of a new assistant, Polly Thomson, she continued to spread hope around the globe. When soldiers in World War II were blinded in battle, Helen visited them in the hospital. When the American Foundation for the Blind was formed, Helen and Polly raised funds for the organization. They visited Scotland, Ireland, South Africa, and the Middle East, speaking to crowds and supporting laws that helped the disabled and disadvantaged.

Polly Thomson died in 1960. Helen was old and fragile herself by then. During the next eight years, Helen suffered a series of strokes and was seldom seen in public, and in 1968, she died. At the time of her death, she had written twelve books and worked for several foundations for the blind. She had given speeches and visited the disabled around the world. She had even been the subject of three movies. Her lifelong determination to succeed and her concern that all others have the chance to live a full life earned Helen Keller the title "America's First Lady of Courage."

Name ____________________

Questions About *America's First Lady of Courage*

1. When Helen Keller was a young girl, why did it seem unlikely that she would become a woman who helped other people?

2. Do you think that the people who gave young Helen money to buy a new dog were upset when she spent the money on something else? Explain why or why not.

3. Why do you think that Helen wanted to write a book about Annie Sullivan?

4. Why did Helen Keller become known as "America's First Lady of Courage"?

5. Although she could not see or hear, Helen Keller did things in her lifetime that many people who can see and hear will never do. List three of her remarkable accomplishments.

Name ______________________________

Vocabulary

Write each word listed below on the line next to its definition.

pantry	tantrum	dignity	fragile
traced	mastered	commission	tutor
Braille	foundation	disabled	stroke

1. ______________________ a sudden stop of blood flowing to the brain
2. ______________________ became very competent or skillful
3. ______________________ a small room for storing food and kitchen supplies
4. ______________________ unable to perform some normal physical activity
5. ______________________ delicate; easily broken
6. ______________________ a group formed to carry out a particular action or duty
7. ______________________ drew a copy of something
8. ______________________ worth and honor
9. ______________________ a private teacher
10. ______________________ an organization that supports a particular cause
11. ______________________ a rant or fit of temper
12. ______________________ a printing system of raised dot patterns that blind people can read with their fingertips

Root Words

A **root word** is the main word, or base word, to which a prefix or a suffix has been added. Write the root word for each word listed below.

1. countless ______________________
2. assistant ______________________
3. earlier ______________________
4. famous ______________________
5. graduation ______________________
6. accomplishments ______________________
7. disadvantaged ______________________
8. organization ______________________

Name ______________________________

Symbolic Actions

Before Helen Keller understood language, she used simple actions to communicate. She pretended to slice and butter a piece of bread when she wanted to eat, or she imitated putting on reading glasses when she wanted her father. What actions would you use to communicate the following information?

1. You are outside and want to go inside.

____

2. You want to go for a drive.

____

3. You want to read a book.

____

4. You want to listen to music.

____

5. You want to watch a movie.

____

6. You want to visit a friend.

____

7. You want to play basketball.

____

8. You want to go shopping.

____

9. You want to go to school.

____

10. You want a drink of water.

____

Name ______________________

Write About It

1. When Helen Keller was a young girl, she felt very frustrated because she was not able to communicate with others. Think about a time when you felt very frustrated. Write about why you were frustrated and how you dealt with your frustration.

2. Helen Keller accomplished a lot more in her lifetime than many people expected of a blind and deaf girl. Think about a time when you surprised yourself or someone else with something you accomplished. Write about your accomplishment and why it was surprising.

The Day Pecos Bill Rode Old Twister

An American Tall Tale

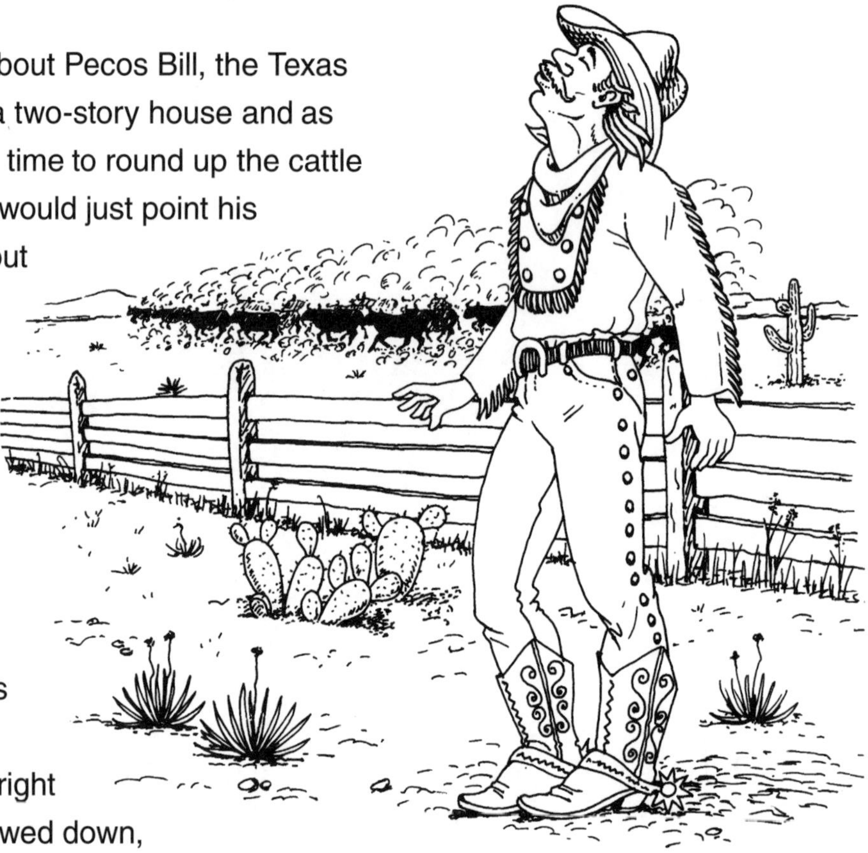

You've probably heard about Pecos Bill, the Texas wrangler who was as tall as a two-story house and as strong as an ox. When it was time to round up the cattle and drive 'em to Abilene, Bill would just point his nose toward the sky and let out a coyote howl that echoed all across Texas. Now, the cattle thought there were a hundred or so coyotes comin' after them, and they were so spooked that they stampeded as fast as they could in the other direction. 'Course Bill had cowpunchers stationed all along the trail to keep the cattle runnin' in the right direction. When the cattle slowed down, Bill just let loose with another howl, and the cattle kept runnin' until they'd all reached Abilene in record time.

You might think it was strange that Bill could howl like that. Well, you see, because coyotes raised him, he came by it naturally. Some folks say Bill thought he was a coyote until he was fourteen years old. Seems he got lost from his folks when they were movin' west. But that's a story for another day.

Bein' pretty much like a coyote, Bill would stop to sniff around every now and then. He could smell almost anything in the air a hundred miles away. One mornin' he said, "Better head for the cellar. There's a twister comin'!" Then Bill put his ear to the ground and announced, "It just passed by El Paso. It's an hour away." That was enough time to get some of the cattle into the tunnel Bill had dug using his pet snake, Rattler, as a drill. As soon as everything was in order, all the cowhands headed for the cellar.

"You comin' in, Bill?" yelled Cowpoke Carl.

"I'm gonna ride this one out!" Bill shouted back, so Carl shut the wood cover to the cellar and bolted it in place.

As for the rest of the story, this here is how Bill told it when he showed up a week or two later. And there's no doubt he was tellin' the truth. Bill was as truthful as a Sunday school teacher.

It seems Bill and his horse, Bulldozer, waited until Old Twister came roarin' across the ranch like an angry panther chasin' its dinner. When the twister caught sight of Bill, it set out after him. Bill led Old Twister away from the barn and the bunkhouse as far as he could. Bulldozer managed to dance to the side each time Twister came close to Bill. That big wind was racin' at such a speed that it could only twirl straight ahead like a ballerina spinnin' across the stage. It couldn't keep up with Bulldozer's fancy sidesteppin'. Old Twister got uglier by the minute. It wasn't used to playin' a losin' game of tag, and it was clear to Bill that Twister wouldn't slow down until it tore up the whole ranch and him along with it.

"I've tamed bears, snakes, and wolves," Bill said to Bulldozer. "I guess it's time I took the fight out of Old Twister, too. My rope's ready, and I'm goin' for the ride of my life. Bulldozer, you head out as far away from this bag a' wind as you can. Leave the rest to me."

Bill threw his rope into the air and sent it whirling faster than a bolt of lightnin'. The lasso dropped over the top of Old Twister and headed for the middle of that windy monster. Bill tightened the rope and gripped the end. Hangin' on like a flea on a dog, he jumped onto the side of the twister and climbed toward the top. Old Twister hopped and danced and nearly turned itself wrong side out tryin' to shake Bill off. It was some fight, but Bill never gave up. He just climbed higher, pokin' his spurs right into the twister's sides.

When Bill reached the top of the twister, he was a little the worse for wear. His hair stood straight up like the points on a picket fence, and his leather shirt was so fringed it looked like blades of brown prairie grass. Nonetheless, he was as calm as a hibernatin' bear. Bill rode bareback on the rim of that twister, lookin' straight down inside it. There was a city's worth of houses, a herd or two of cattle, and pretty much everything else you could need just swirling around in there.

Twister arched its back and kicked up its tail like a buckin' bronco at a rodeo. It didn't do any good, though. Bill rode Old Twister like he was a kid ridin' on a rockin' horse. He was havin' so much fun that he decided there oughta be some good done along the way. It was a shame to let Old Twister smash up all those houses. People movin' west had a long stretch to travel without comin' to a town, so Bill reached down inside the whirlwind and pulled out the houses one by one. As he tossed the houses behind the twister, they settled down in neat rows, makin' up the prettiest town you could imagine. Now people'd have a place to stop and rest when they crossed that long, dry stretch of prairie.

Bill scooped up all the grass and plants inside the twister, too, and threw 'em into a giant stack near the town. Each time the twister tried to roar off across the prairie, Bill just dug in his spurs, and while the twister spun around in circles going nowhere, Bill scooped out the cattle and dropped 'em onto the stack of grass so they'd have enough to eat until the next wagon train came rumblin' along. When he was finished, Bill had made a fine place to settle down, and he told himself that, one day, he'd do just that.

Old Twister was empty now and as tired as a mother hen that had spent the day chasin' after her chicks. It was nothin' but a little breeze and as gentle as a newborn lamb frolickin' across a meadow. As for Bill, he'd had enough travelin' for a while, so he just went back to ridin' Bulldozer around the ranch and howlin' at the moon.

Name ____________________

Questions About *The Day Pecos Bill Rode Old Twister*

1. How did Pecos Bill drive the cattle to Abilene?

2. How did Pecos Bill learn to howl like a coyote?

3. How did Pecos Bill know there was a twister coming?

4. How did Pecos Bill catch the twister?

5. What made Pecos Bill think that the twister wouldn't stop until it tore up the whole ranch?

6. What did Pecos Bill do with the houses and the cattle that were caught up in the twister?

7. What finally happened to the twister?

Name ______________________________

The Day Pecos Bill Rode Old Twister

Vocabulary Crossword

Use the words in the word box to complete the crossword puzzle.

Word Box

bareback
bolted
bronco
bunkhouse
cellar
fringed
frolicking
lasso
panther
sidestepping
spooked
spurs
stampeded
stationed
stretch
twister
wrangler

Across

2. rushed forward wildly as a group
5. having thin strips hanging from the edges
6. positioned at a certain place
7. a rope with a noose that is used to catch horses and cattle
9. a building that has rows of beds or cots for cowboys to sleep on
12. a cowboy who herds horses or cattle
13. a large, black wild cat
14. a long or wide piece of land

Down

1. on a horse without a saddle
2. moving from side to side to avoid one or more obstacles
3. a wild horse
4. an underground storage area
5. running and playing merrily; romping
8. frightened
9. ran off quickly and suddenly
10. sharp-edged metal disks that are worn on the heels of cowboy boots
11. a whirling funnel-shaped windstorm

Name ____________________________

The Day Pecos Bill Rode Old Twister

Similes

A **simile** is a figure of speech that describes a person or an action by comparing it to something completely different. The comparison uses the words **like** or **as.**

Examples: *Pecos Bill* was as strong **as** an ox. (describes a person)
He *howled* **like** a coyote. (describes an action)

Find phrases in the story that contain similes for each of the following sentences.

1. Pecos Bill was truthful.

 ____

2. Pecos Bill was tall.

 ____

3. Bill's hair stood straight up.

 ____

4. His shirt was fringed.

 ____

5. Bill was calm.

 ____

6. The twister arched its back and kicked up its tail.

 ____

7. The twister turned into a little breeze.

 ____

8. Old Twister came roaring across the ranch.

 ____

Name ____________________

Exaggeration

Tall tales are stories that contain exaggerated descriptions and actions that readers know are not true to life or cannot happen in real life.

Examples: Pecos Bill let out a howl that echoed all across Texas.
No human sound is loud enough to be heard across such a distance.

Bill rode Old Twister like he was a kid ridin' on a rockin' horse.
A person cannot ride on wind and would be injured or killed trying.

Find five more exaggerations in the story and explain why they are not true to life or cannot happen.

1. ____________________

2. ____________________

3. ____________________

4. ____________________

5. ____________________

Picturing History

The Story of Mathew Brady and His Camera

Mathew Brady was fascinated with the new camera portraits being taken in France in the late 1830s. They were called *daguerreotypes* (deh-**gehr**-uh-tipes). While working at other jobs, Brady studied chemistry and learned everything he could from people who knew how to take these photo portraits. In 1844, he opened a studio in New York City and began doing this kind of photography himself.

Until daguerreotypes, portraits had to be painted by artists. Often, the artist would improve how the subject looked in order to charge more money for the portrait. Shot with a camera, portraits were true to life, but making daguerreotypes was very difficult.

The photographer first had to prepare a silver surface, or plate. The plate was exposed to iodine vapors to make it sensitive to light. Then the plate had to be kept away from light until it was time to take the picture. To get an image on the plate, the surface had to be exposed to light at just the right time and for the right amount of time. The person being photographed had to sit motionless for up to 30 minutes while his or her image "burned" onto the plate. Then the plate had to be covered again quickly and taken to a darkroom.

Working in dim candlelight, the photographer placed the plate in a box and exposed it to heated mercury. After the image appeared, it was fixed with a salt solution. The picture was very delicate. Even brushing against it with a soft cloth could rub away the image. To protect the image, the picture was put inside a glass box. If an image was damaged or had turned out too light or too dark, there was no way to fix it. The whole process had to be done again.

Many famous people came to Mathew Brady to have their pictures taken. Except for William Henry Harrison, Brady photographed all of the U.S. presidents from John Quincy Adams to William McKinley. He took many photos of Abraham Lincoln. In fact, a portrait of Lincoln is one of Brady's most well-known pictures.

Singers, actors, and authors also came to Brady to be photographed. Even King Edward VII of England took time for a portrait at Brady's studio when he stopped in New York on his way to Canada. In the 1850s, Brady opened another studio in Washington, D.C., and had to start hiring assistants to help with the workload. Brady also needed the assistants because his eyesight, which had always been poor, was getting worse.

In 1861, when the American Civil War began, Brady thought that taking pictures was important to preserve the war for history. Because the pictures had to be developed right after they were taken, Brady carted his equipment, his darkroom, and his assistants to battlefields and army camps. When the Union Army retreated in the battle of Bull Run, Brady's wagon was destroyed, forcing him and his crew to make their way back to Washington, D.C., on foot. Even so, Brady and his assistants continued to photograph battles that took place near the nation's capital.

Brady's Civil War pictures were published in books, but few people bought the books. At the time, people didn't want to be reminded of the war. Because Brady had spent so much time and money on those photos, his studios began to fail. To save his photography business, he tried to sell the Civil War collection to the government. In 1871, Congress agreed to buy 2,000 photographs but didn't set aside money for the purchase.

Unable to pay his debts, Brady lost his New York studio. He was able, however, to carry out many loads of portraits and photographs before sheriff's deputies arrived to evict him. He managed to keep his other studio and continue his work in Washington, D.C. Although the government finally paid him $25,000 for many of his pictures, Brady had to close his remaining studio in 1881.

Despite his popularity and his contributions to 19th-century history, award-winning photographer Mathew Brady died alone and penniless in 1896. Many of his photos did not survive, either. The government did not take care of the plates it had purchased from Brady and would not pay to restore the damaged collection. As a result, many priceless historical photo-documents were lost forever.

Today, when we see copies of the Brady photos that have survived, we know what Abraham Lincoln and many other famous people really looked like. We also see actual scenes from the American Civil War because Mathew Brady was there with his assistants and his camera.

Name ______________________

Questions About *Picturing History*

1. Before cameras were invented, how did people get pictures of themselves?

2. What were some of the challenges in making a daguerreotype? List at least three.

3. Why might Mathew Brady have been considered a reporter for the Civil War?

4. Why didn't people want to buy Brady's books of Civil War pictures?

5. Why was Brady's work with the camera important?

6. Name the advancement in today's photography that you think would surprise Brady the most.

Name ______________________________

Vocabulary

A. Write each word listed below on the line next to its definition.

carted	preserve	exposed	plate	restore	darkroom
image	evict	daguerreotypes	portrait	mercury	studio

1. ______________________ a head and shoulders picture of a person
2. ______________________ to bring back to brand-new condition
3. ______________________ a picture or likeness of someone or something
4. ______________________ a chemical element that is often seen as a silvery liquid
5. ______________________ a flat, thin sheet of a hard material such as metal or glass
6. ______________________ pictures made using a very early photographic method
7. ______________________ the main work area of an artist or a photographer
8. ______________________ to keep from being lost or destroyed
9. ______________________ a place with no light rays to damage photo images
10. ______________________ carried or moved as if in a small wagon
11. ______________________ left out in the open, unprotected
12. ______________________ to remove from a rented property by legal means

B. Read each pair of definitions below. Write the word they define on the line and fill in the circle next to the definition used in the story.

1. ______________________ Ⓐ set or fastened firmly in place
   Ⓑ repaired or mended
2. ______________________ Ⓐ the answer to a problem
   Ⓑ a mixture of a solid dissolved in a liquid

Name ______________________________

Sequencing

A. Write the missing steps for making a daguerreotype.

1. Prepare a silver surface, or plate.
2. ______________________________
3. Expose the plate to light.
4. ______________________________
5. ______________________________
6. ______________________________
7. Expose the plate to heated mercury.
8. ______________________________
9. ______________________________

B. List, in order, each of the seven dates that appear in the story and write a brief description of what happened at or around that time.

______ ______________________________

______ ______________________________

______ ______________________________

______ ______________________________

______ ______________________________

______ ______________________________

______ ______________________________

Name ____________________

Problems and Solutions

For each problem below, write Mathew Brady's solution.

1. **Problem:** The only way to have a portrait done was to hire an artist to paint one.

   Solution: ____________________

2. **Problem:** An image that was "burned" onto the plate would be damaged by light until it was fixed with a salt solution.

   Solution: ____________________

3. **Problem:** An image turned out too light or too dark.

   Solution: ____________________

4. **Problem:** Brady's workload increased greatly in the 1850s.

   Solution: ____________________

5. **Problem:** Any photographs that Brady took on a battlefield or in an army camp had to be developed immediately.

   Solution: ____________________

6. **Problem:** No one bought Brady's books of Civil War photographs.

   Solution: ____________________

Write About It

Write an argument that Brady could have used to convince the United States government to buy his photos of the Civil War.

____

____

____

____

____

Jackie Robinson

Jack Roosevelt Robinson was born in Georgia in 1919. He was the youngest of five children, and when "Jackie," as he was called, was only six months old, his mother moved the family to Pasadena, California, hoping to find a better life.

Jackie didn't have much time for play while he was growing up. He was busy delivering newspapers, running errands, and cutting lawns to earn money. The Robinson family was poor, and Jackie had to help out. On weekends, he sold hot dogs at a nearby baseball stadium, but what he noticed there bothered him. None of the teams had any black players.

In high school, Robinson played baseball, basketball, and football. He also ran track. He participated in the same sports in college, and at the University of California at Los Angeles (UCLA), he became the first athlete ever to win awards in all four of them.

Robinson left UCLA in 1941 to take a job as the assistant athletic director for a government-sponsored youth program. Later that year, the attack on Pearl Harbor forced the United States into World War II, and in 1942, Robinson was drafted into the army. During his tour of duty, he wanted to join the army's baseball and football teams, but because he was black, the army would not allow it. He did, however, serve for a short time as an army athletic coach.

After completing his military duty in 1944, Robinson briefly played football and coached basketball. Then, in 1945, he received an offer from the Kansas City Monarchs to play professional baseball in the Negro American League. Robinson was skilled enough to play major league baseball, but the major league teams hired only white players. Fortunately for Robinson, a brave man named Branch Rickey was about to change all that. In 1946, Rickey, who was the president of the Brooklyn Dodgers, signed Robinson to play for the Dodgers' minor league team, the Montreal Royals. The very next year, Rickey signed Robinson to play first base for the Dodgers.

Being the first black player in major league baseball since the 1880s took a lot of courage. Many players and fans did not want Robinson on a major league team, but his determination and skill paid off. In 1947, he was named Rookie of the Year. In 1949, he was the MVP (Most Valuable Player). And in 1955, he helped the Brooklyn Dodgers win their first World Series.

Although Robinson retired from playing baseball in 1957, he was honored again in 1962, when he became the first black player to be voted into baseball's Hall of Fame. No one deserved this honor more. Robinson was a great athlete and one of the greatest baseball players of all time. He was also a great man who helped pave the way for other black players in the major leagues.

Even after baseball, Robinson did a lot to help other black Americans. As a successful businessman, he raised money for the National Association for the Advancement of Colored People (NAACP) and served as a board member for that organization for many years. He also helped found Freedom National Bank, which was owned and operated by African Americans, and he established a construction company to build houses for low-income families. Just as he had distinguished himself in baseball, Robinson also distinguished himself in the business world. He was the first black person to become vice president of a major American corporation.

October 15, 1972, was the twenty-fifth anniversary of Jackie Robinson's first game as a major league baseball player. He was awarded a plaque in honor of the event and threw out the first pitch at the second game of the 1972 World Series. Less than two weeks later, on October 24, Robinson had a heart attack at his home and died. More than two thousand people attended his funeral service, and tens of thousands stood along the route to the cemetery where he was buried.

A few months before Robinson died, the Brooklyn Dodgers retired his uniform number 42. On April 15, 1997, all of major league baseball retired the number 42, which means that no player on any major league baseball team can ever wear that number again. This kind of tribute was a first in American major league sports and another first for Jack Roosevelt "Jackie" Robinson.

Questions About *Jackie Robinson*

1. How did Jackie Robinson spend a lot of his time while he was growing up?

2. Most of today's major league baseball players start their careers right out of college. Why didn't Jackie Robinson's baseball career start right after college?

3. List three things that Jackie Robinson was the first to accomplish.

4. What are some ways that, as a businessman, Jackie Robinson helped other black Americans?

5. Why were October 15, 1972, and April 15, 1997, important days for Jackie Robinson?

Name ______________________

Jackie Robinson

Vocabulary

Write the number of each word on the line next to its meaning.

1. determination	_____	recognized as different or outstanding
2. tribute	_____	the state of being well-known or honored
3. fame	_____	of great worth or importance
4. plaque	_____	the quality of sticking to a purpose
5. distinguished	_____	selected or called to perform military service
6. drafted	_____	a special show of respect or recognition
7. valuable	_____	had costs paid by an outside individual or organization
8. sponsored	_____	a flat piece of inscribed wood or metal that recognizes an event or an accomplishment

Sports Word Search

Find and circle 12 sports-related words from the story in the word search puzzle below. Then write the words alphabetically on the lines to make a word list.

b	a	s	e	b	a	l	l	b	s	e	w
a	c	k	a	t	h	l	e	t	e	m	t
n	x	s	b	k	a	m	a	k	f	c	e
s	l	t	c	b	r	j	g	w	u	c	a
y	m	s	t	a	d	i	u	m	n	o	m
b	w	o	r	l	d	s	e	r	i	e	s
t	o	i	b	u	h	l	s	o	f	s	e
f	n	u	s	c	h	u	b	o	o	t	r
a	p	m	a	t	r	a	c	k	r	u	i
n	t	o	l	m	s	a	v	i	m	h	w
s	c	n	o	p	c	h	r	e	p	s	e

Word List

____

____

____

____

____

____

____

____

____

____

____

____

Name ____________________

Jackie Robinson

What Does It Mean?

A. An **expression** is an unusual but commonly used way of saying something. Use your own words to explain the meanings of these expressions from the story.

1. tour of duty

____

2. pave the way

____

B. The word **retired** has two meanings in the story. Write both meanings below. Use a dictionary if you need help.

1. ____________________

2. ____________________

Think About It

Explain why you think the author said that being the first black player in major league baseball took a lot of courage.

____

____

____

____

____

____

____

____

____

____

Name ______________________________

Jackie Robinson

Topics and Details

Write details under each of these topics from the story. Write one detail next to each letter. The details do not have to be complete sentences.

I. Childhood

A. ______________________________

B. ______________________________

C. ______________________________

II. High School and College

A. ______________________________

B. ______________________________

III. Sports Career

A. ______________________________

B. ______________________________

C. ______________________________

D. ______________________________

IV. Business Career

A. ______________________________

B. ______________________________

C. ______________________________

V. Awards and Honors

A. ______________________________

B. ______________________________

C. ______________________________

D. ______________________________

Love That Chocolate!

Drop a spoonful of powdered chocolate into milk. Spread chocolate frosting on a graham cracker. Drizzle chocolate syrup over ice cream. Celebrate a holiday with foil-wrapped chocolate coins, a chocolate Santa, or a cream-filled chocolate egg. Better yet, open a box of aromatic chocolates with soft, gooey, or chewy centers—after dinner, of course.

Wait! Even if you ate all your vegetables, don't scoop up those chocolates just yet. Take a deep breath or two—or three! Enjoy the tantalizing smell. Next, survey the chocolate circles, squares, and rectangles. Which ones are hiding your favorite creams, nuts, or caramels? No fair poking holes in the bottoms to find the ones you want. Be adventurous! You can always try again if you don't get what you expected. Just be careful that you don't eat them all. You'll want to save some for tomorrow.

From Cacao Trees to Cocoa Beans

Chocolate comes from cacao trees, most of which are grown on large plantations. Although native to Mexico, cacao trees now grow all over the world in the tropical zones near the equator. They thrive where temperatures are in the 80s all year round and never drop below about 60° Fahrenheit (16° Celsius).

In the wild, cacao trees can grow up to 50 feet (15 meters) tall. On plantations, they are pruned to be no taller than 25 feet (8 m). Pods full of cocoa beans hang from the trunk and branches of the tree. Blossoms form throughout the year, and football-shaped pods develop from the flowers. It takes five to six months for a pod to change in color from green to a ripe purple. When the pod is ripe, it can be harvested.

Cacao pods are usually harvested twice a year, in fall and in spring. Each pod has 20 to 40 white, almond-sized seeds (cocoa beans) inside, surrounded by white pulp. At this stage, the cocoa beans and the pulp taste bitter. A lot of processing goes into creating that mouthwatering chocolate flavor you enjoy when you bite into a chocolate chip cookie.

First, the seeds and pulp are cut out of the pod. Then, they are either heated or left in the hot sun. Heat turns the pulp into a liquid, which is drained off the beans so that the beans will dry. After the beans are thoroughly dried, they turn a dark brown color. The smell and flavor of the beans is now more like the sweet odor of chocolate in a candy bar—but it isn't chocolate yet!

Chocolate at Last!

Cocoa beans are shipped to candy factories all over the world. There, the beans are brushed clean and roasted. The outer shells of the beans are removed either before or after roasting. The inside of a cocoa bean is called a *nib*. After cocoa nibs are roasted, they're crushed. The heat of the crushing process melts the cocoa butter in the nibs. Depending on how much melted cocoa butter is removed, different types of rich chocolate paste remain and are processed further to make different types of chocolate.

Sometimes, the chocolate paste is used to make hard brown blocks of unsweetened baking chocolate, or the paste might be mixed with sugar, milk, and other ingredients to make melt-in-your-mouth chocolate bars and candies. It might even be used to flavor a truckload of rocky road ice cream or be added to bitter medicines to make them taste better.

Chocolate Conquers the World

Long before people from Europe settled in the Americas, the Native Americans enjoyed chocolate. They used chocolate to make a special drink for royalty. The Aztec kings added chocolate to a mixture of seasonings and corn mash to make a bitter, peppery tasting beverage. Sometimes, they added honey, vanilla, and chili peppers to the drink, too. Chocolate was so valuable to the Native Americans that it was often used as money in the marketplace.

When Spanish explorers brought cocoa beans back to Spain, they used the beans to make a drink that became popular with the royal family and the nobles of the Spanish court. Wooden beaters were used to whip the chocolate until it was foamy, and then sugar was added to the drink. Orange water, white rose powder, cloves, and other spices were also mixed into the chocolate.

The Spaniards tried to keep chocolate a secret, but eventually, visitors to the royal court took the drink back to their own countries. In the 1600s, its popularity spread across Europe. One hundred years later, chocolate was shipped from England to the British colonists in North America. The colonists became very fond of chocolate drinks, and their doctors prescribed chocolate for energy and good health.

Chocolate in Your Diet

During World War II, soldiers ate chocolate bars to add extra calories to their diets. The extra calories gave them more energy. Explorers in cold climates also eat chocolate for energy. The calories from the chocolate help them stay active. For most people, however, chocolate should be eaten only occasionally and in small amounts. It is a good source of minerals and vitamin B, but, like coffee, it contains caffeine, which can keep you awake when your body needs rest.

In almost all forms, chocolate is very rich and has a lot of calories. One small chocolate bar has about the same number of calories as two bananas, two slices of cheese, or three slices of white bread, but more of the chocolate bar's calories typically come from fat. Nevertheless, chocolate is enjoyed in great quantities throughout the world. People just love that chocolate!

Name ______________________________

Questions about *Love That Chocolate!*

1. What do cacao trees have to do with chocolate?

____

____

2. Where do the pods grow on a cacao tree? ______________________

3. How long does it take for a cacao pod to ripen, and how can you recognize a ripe pod?

____

4. Could you grow a cacao tree where you live? Explain why or why not.

____

____

5. Chocolate was first enjoyed by the Aztecs as a drink. What ingredients did the Aztecs add to the chocolate?

____

6. What ingredients did the Spanish use to make chocolate drinks?

____

7. What is a *nib*, and how are nibs used to make different types of chocolate?

____

____

____

8. What fact about chocolate were you surprised to learn?

____

____

Name ___________________________

Love That Chocolate!

Vocabulary

A. Use these words from the story to complete the analogies below.

aromatic caffeine drizzle plantations pods survey tropical

1. **Peanuts** are to **shells** as **cocoa beans** are to ______________________.
2. **Apples** are to **orchards** as **cacao trees** are to ______________________.
3. **Ice-cold** is to **polar** as **hot** is to ______________________.
4. **Smelly** is to **stinky** as **fragrant** is to ______________________.
5. **Smear** is to **spread** as **trickle** is to ______________________.
6. **Vitamin C** is to **oranges** as ______________________ is to **coffee**.
7. **Listen** is to **ears** as ______________________ is to **eyes**.

B. Use each of these words in a complete sentence to answer the questions below. **Hint:** Two words can be used in the same sentence.

cacao equator harvested native pulp tantalizing zones

1. Where did cacao trees originate?

____

2. Where do cacao trees grow best?

____

3. Where are cocoa beans found?

____

4. What happens to ripe cacao pods?

____

5. What is one reason that people are tempted to eat chocolate?

____

Name ___________________________

Create a Candy Bar

A. List adjectives on the lines below that describe the taste and texture of chocolate.

Examples: sweet *(taste)* buttery *(texture)*

Taste	Texture
______________	______________
______________	______________
______________	______________
______________	______________
______________	______________

B. Create your own chocolate candy bar and draw it in the space below. Give the candy bar a name and a wrapper that will appeal to kids. Under your drawing, list some of the ingredients and write a description of your candy bar that would convince someone to try it. Use some of the adjectives listed above.

Ingredients:	**Description:**
______________	______________
______________	______________
______________	______________
______________	______________
______________	______________

Name ______________________________

Main Ideas and Details

The subheads in the story give clues about each section's main idea. Under each subhead below, list four important details that support that section's main idea.

1. From Cacao Trees to Cocoa Beans

   a. ______________________________

   b. ______________________________

   c. ______________________________

   d. ______________________________

2. Chocolate at Last!

   a. ______________________________

   b. ______________________________

   c. ______________________________

   d. ______________________________

3. Chocolate Conquers the World

   a. ______________________________

   b. ______________________________

   c. ______________________________

   d. ______________________________

4. Chocolate in Your Diet

   a. ______________________________

   b. ______________________________

   c. ______________________________

   d. ______________________________

Laurence Yep

Author Laurence Yep grew up in a world of cereal boxes, raw liver, pickles in a barrel, soda bottles, and penny bubble gum. His parents owned a grocery store in San Francisco. Everyone in the family worked long hours in the store. Laurence and his older brother, Thomas, stocked shelves, sorted bottles, and flattened boxes. They had to mark prices on the groceries, too. The Yeps lived very close to where they worked. Their apartment on the corner of Pierce and Eddy Streets was directly above the store.

The grocery store was open seven days a week, but when they could get away from the store, the Yeps enjoyed picnics and other outdoor activities together. Mr. Yep made butterfly kites for them to fly, or they would go to the beach to wade in the water and gather sand. Mr. Yep had built a sandbox on the roof of their building. That sandbox is where Laurence created his first imaginary kingdoms.

The Yeps were a Chinese American family. Laurence's father was born in China. He came to the United States at the age of ten. Laurence's mother had always lived in the United States. She was born in Ohio and was raised in West Virginia and California.

Many Chinese Americans in San Francisco lived in the Chinatown district, where the Chinese language and Chinese customs were part of everyday life. Because they lived so traditionally, however, people from Chinatown weren't always welcome in other parts of San Francisco.

The Yep family did not live in Chinatown. Their store was in a different part of the city, and many of their neighbors were African Americans, rather than Chinese Americans. Although his family frequently visited friends and relatives in Chinatown, and Laurence even went to school there, he still seemed to feel more American than Chinese while he was growing up. Often, he felt as if he didn't belong in either culture. Many of Yep's stories reflect those feelings. The stories are about people who must learn to adjust to new places and to people who have different customs.

Yep's passion for stories and books began long before he started writing his own. Because his parents felt that education was very important, they read stories to their children and had the children read to them. Laurence's favorite stories took place in the Land of Oz. He searched for books about Oz in the library and read them all. Next, he read every science-fiction book he could find.

Laurence understood how the characters in the Oz books and the aliens in science-fiction stories felt. They were thrust into strange worlds where they didn't belong, which was how he felt about being Chinese and American. While he was going to school in Chinatown, Yep excelled in most subjects, especially science, but he didn't like learning Chinese. Most of his schoolmates spoke Chinese at home and were in the advanced classes. Yep's family spoke only English at home, so the Chinese class that Laurence had to take was for beginners, and he was often made fun of or felt left out.

When Yep started high school, his parents wanted him to have more time to study, so he stopped working long hours at the grocery store. His favorite classes were in science. He planned to study chemistry in college. But he did well in his English writing classes, too. Before he graduated high school, English had won out over chemistry, and Yep decided to study journalism in college.

Yep left California to attend Marquette University in Wisconsin. Although homesick for San Francisco, he did well in all of his classes except journalism. One of his teachers suggested that he might do better writing fiction than reporting facts. That teacher was right, and Yep's career as a published writer began with the first science-fiction story he wrote. The story was "The Selchey Kids." It was published in *If* magazine, and Yep was paid a penny a word.

At Marquette, Yep met Joanne Ryder, a student editor for the school's literary magazine. Ryder introduced Yep to children's books, and when she later became a children's book editor for a New York publisher, she asked Yep to write a children's book and send it to her. Yep wrote the science-fiction story *Sweetwater.* It was his first novel, and Ryder was his editor. The novel was published in 1973.

Yep continued to write books for children and young adults and has won many awards for books about Chinese Americans. Today, Laurence Yep and Joanne Ryder are married to each other, and both are well-known authors of books for children and young adults.

A Selection of Young Adult Novels by Laurence Yep

Sweetwater (1973)
*Dragonwings (1975)
Child of the Owl (1977)
Sea Glass (1979)
Dragon of the Lost Sea (1982)
Kind Hearts and Gentle Monsters (1982)
The Serpent's Children (1984)
Mountain Light (1985)
The Rainbow People (1989)
The Lost Garden (1991)
Tongues of Jade (1991)
Dragon War (1992)
*Dragon's Gate (1993)
The Ghost Fox (1994)
Later, Gator (1995)
Thief of Hearts (1995)
The Case of the Goblin Pearls (1997)
The Amah (1999)
The Magic Paintbrush (2000)
The Tiger's Apprentice (2003)
Dragon Road (2008)
City of Fire (2009)
The Star Maker (2010)

**Newbery Honor winners*

Name ______________________________

Questions About *Laurence Yep*

1. How did Yep's parents influence his eventual career as an author?

___

___

___

2. Why do you think that Yep felt more American than Chinese?

___

___

___

3. As a boy and as a young adult what kinds of books did Yep most like to read? Why?

___

___

4. Why didn't Yep pursue a career in journalism?

___

___

5. What was the name of Yep's first children's novel? Why did he write it?

___

___

___

6. Newbery Honors are awarded to books that are considered important contributions to American children's literature. Which books written by Laurence Yep are Newbery Honor winners?

___

Name ______________________________

Laurence Yep

Vocabulary

Write the number of each word on the line next to its meaning.

1. custom	______	an area within a city that has a specific use or purpose
2. editor	______	a person who gathers and reports the news
3. district	______	put in a supply of goods
4. literary	______	a strong attraction to or powerful feeling for something
5. passion	______	a practice or routine among people of the same culture
6. journalist	______	relating to books or writing
7. excel	______	a person who corrects and revises written materials
8. stocked	______	to do something better than most others do it

Fantasy Word Search

Find each word listed in the word box and circle it in the puzzle.

Word Box	
aliens	monster
angel	Oz
dragon	rainbow
imaginary	science fiction
kingdoms	serpent
magic	Sweetwater

v	m	s	e	r	p	e	n	t
i	w	c	t	v	l	e	t	e
m	k	i	n	g	d	o	m	s
a	t	e	a	i	r	g	l	w
g	z	n	o	n	a	e	r	e
i	k	c	m	a	g	i	c	e
n	c	e	m	n	o	e	o	t
a	e	f	o	i	n	b	l	w
r	a	i	n	b	o	w	k	a
y	o	c	s	h	z	s	m	t
o	v	t	t	c	r	z	m	e
a	l	i	e	n	s	c	h	r
d	m	o	r	a	t	s	n	g
k	e	n	a	i	z	e	s	t

Name ______________________

Think About It

A. Imagine that you are a journalist assigned to write an article about Laurence Yep. On the lines below, write five questions you would ask Mr. Yep in an interview to find out information that was not in the story.

1. ______________________

2. ______________________

3. ______________________

4. ______________________

5. ______________________

B. A character in Yep's book *Dragon's Gate* says, "You can learn to change the world..." Yep changed his world by creating new worlds as a fantasy and science-fiction writer. How could you change your world?

____

Name ______________________________

Write About It

Laurence Yep created his first imaginary kingdoms in a sandbox. Later, he created them in his stories. Imaginary kingdoms or magical worlds in faraway places and distant times are key elements of **fantasy**. Other elements of fantasy include characters and objects with special powers and a conflict between good and evil.

Create your own imaginary or fantasy kingdom by describing each element below. Start by giving your kingdom a name.

Name of kingdom: ______________________________

Description of kingdom (include time period and place): ______________________________

____

____

____

____

____

____

Main characters and their powers: ______________________________

____

____

____

Summary of conflict: ______________________________

____

____

____

____

Let's Celebrate

Lisa looked out her bedroom window and watched her mom and her cousin Elena carry suitcases into the house. Elena had come from Mexico to stay with them for the rest of the school year. Her parents wanted her to live in the United States for a while so she could practice her English.

"Sixth grade won't be much fun anymore," Lisa thought. "I'll be doing nothing but homework every afternoon and evening. After I help Elena with hers, I'll have to do my own, and I won't ever have time to watch TV or visit my friends or do anything fun. I'm happy that Elena already speaks English so at least we'll be able to understand each other, I think."

Since Elena was arriving at almost the end of October and had already missed the first part of the school year, Mom insisted that Lisa give up her after-school activities.

"I can't be driving back and forth all the time," Mom had told Lisa, "and it wouldn't be fair to make Elena wait for you to finish play practice, so I'll have to pick you both up right after school."

Lisa had a big part in the school play *Let's Celebrate*, but she hadn't yet told Mr. Blake, the director, that she couldn't come to rehearsals anymore. She was hoping that Mom might still change her mind.

"Well, here we are," Mom said, as she led Elena into the bedroom and put the suitcases down next to the bed that Elena would be using while she was there. "I'll leave you two to get acquainted. Lisa, you can help Elena unpack."

"But Mom," Lisa pleaded. "I was going to help you make something special for dinner. I think we should welcome Elena with a good, home-cooked American meal, don't you?"

"Not tonight," Mom said, leaving the room. "Dad's bringing pizza home with him, so Elena will see how we normally eat around here."

"I am very glad that you are in this room with me," said Elena. "In Mexico, my three sisters and I all sleep together in the same room. We do everything together! We are very close. We will be good friends, you and I—no?"

"Well, we'll be together a lot. That's for sure," Lisa answered quickly. "Come on, let's start unpacking."

Lisa watched as Elena opened the biggest suitcase. The first things Elena took out of the suitcase were pictures and candles.

"I brought things for *Día de los Muertos* (**mwer**-tohs), the Day of the Dead," she said. "My mother sent them with me so your family can make an altar for our grandfather."

"We don't celebrate the Day of the Dead," said Lisa.

"But I saw skeletons in many windows when we were driving here from the airport," Elena responded.

"Oh, the skeletons..." Lisa replied. "They're for Halloween! It's a fun holiday for kids, and part of the fun is decorating houses and yards with skeletons, ghosts, bats, spiders, and lots of other creepy stuff."

Lisa took some clothes out of Elena's suitcase and put them in the dresser drawers her mom had emptied to make room for Elena's things.

"Mom told me about the Day of the Dead," Lisa continued, "but I didn't understand all of it. Some of Mom's friends have altars in their houses for family members who have died, but Mom doesn't do that, maybe because my dad is from England. I'm sure we celebrate holidays a lot differently at our house from what you do in Mexico."

"Everything will be strange here, I think," said Elena, setting the pictures and candles on top of the dresser. "I will miss being with my family for the Day of the Dead holidays."

"Holidays? You mean the Day of the Dead is more than one day?" Lisa asked.

"It begins on the last day of October and ends on the second day of November," Elena told Lisa. "For three days, we invite the souls of our ancestors to visit us. We clean up the cemetery and decorate it with many flowers, and then we put out some food in our homes and in the cemetery to honor the dead. Look! I have brought this special candy to share."

Elena showed Lisa a box of sugar skeletons and chocolate skulls. Then she pulled out another box.

"I have also brought *pan de muertos,*" said Elena. "It is bread for the dead. My mother baked it, but I decorated it with bones. You can give the bread to your mother to save."

Lisa looked at the bones and skull frosting on the bread. "It looks good," she said. "Let's show it to Mom. Bring that other stuff, too."

Elena picked up the pictures and candles and followed Lisa downstairs.

"Hey, Mom, look at this bread," said Lisa. "Elena brought it for the Day of the Dead. She brought pictures and candles, too. I guess it's a pretty special holiday for her."

Mom looked at the bread, and then she smiled and put her arm around Elena.

"I guess I'd forgotten just how special it is," she said, giving Elena's shoulders a squeeze. "I've lived in the United States for such a long time that I've lost track of most of the Mexican holidays I used to celebrate. But many Mexican Americans celebrate those holidays here, and I still enjoy watching the parades and the dancing on Cinco de Mayo. I think I'd like to start celebrating more of the Mexican days again, and I'd like to remember my dad. Maybe we should have an altar this year. Several of our neighbors always set up altars on the first day of November."

Lisa and Elena watched Mom as she started to arrange the candles and the pictures Elena had brought on a long cabinet in the dining room.

"On *Día de los Muertos*," Mom went on, "we'll put out some of the foods your grandpa liked, and we can invite friends to share dinner with us."

"Well, since we're talking about holidays, Mom," said Lisa, "wouldn't it be nice for Elena to learn about the ones we celebrate in the United States? The play we're doing at school is about all the holidays in the year—Thanksgiving, the Fourth of July—all of them! If Elena was in the play, then she could find out about our holidays and practice her English at the same time!"

"Oh, could I?" Elena asked. "I would like to be in the play very much."

"Well, Mom?" Lisa asked with a grin.

"Well..." Mom said hesitantly. Then she grinned back at Lisa. "If Mr. Blake agrees, I'll pick you both up from school *after* rehearsal."

Name ________________________________

Questions About *Let's Celebrate*

1. Why was Elena going to stay in the United States for a while?

2. Give two reasons why Lisa wasn't sure she would enjoy Elena's visit.

3. Why did Lisa's mom change her mind about Lisa being in the school play?

4. Describe how Elena's family celebrated the Day of the Dead.

5. Many countries celebrate special days to remember those who have died. Why do you think these holidays exist? What is the name of the holiday in the United States that honors people who have died?

Name ______________________

Vocabulary

Write each word listed below on the line next to its definition.

cemetery	acquainted	honor	rehearsals	pleaded
altar	insisted	souls	cabinet	arrange

1. the unseen spiritual parts of human beings ______________
2. a place where the dead are buried ______________
3. made an urgent request; begged ______________
4. a piece of furniture with a cupboard-like storage area ______________
5. scheduled times for practicing a play or a performance ______________
6. informed about or familiar with ______________
7. a special place at which to honor a departed spirit ______________
8. to show high respect, regard, or recognition ______________
9. stated firmly; demanded ______________
10. to place in a certain order ______________

Antonyms

Find an antonym in the story for each word below and write it on the line.

1. morning ______________
2. remembered ______________
3. familiar ______________
4. filled ______________
5. enemies ______________
6. upstairs ______________
7. separate ______________
8. shame ______________
9. led ______________
10. frowned ______________
11. leaving ______________
12. closed ______________

Name ______________________

Helping Verbs

A. **Helping verbs** are forms of the verbs **be**, **have**, and **do**. They are paired with action verbs to set the time of the action or to make the meaning clearer. *Am*, *is*, *are*, *was*, *were*, *had*, *has*, *have*, *will*, *would*, *did*, *do*, *can*, and *could* are common helping verbs.

Examples: I **will** *bake* a cake. (sets the time of the action in the future)
I **had** *baked* a cake. (sets the time of the action in the past)

Read each sentence below. Draw one line under the action verb and two lines under the helping verb.

1. Elena had come from Mexico.
2. Dad is bringing pizza home with him.
3. You can give the bread to your mother.
4. Elena will miss her family.
5. Lisa was hoping to stay in the play.

B. Sometimes, a helping verb is part of a contraction.

Example: I **am** leaving tomorrow.
I'm leaving tomorrow.

Rewrite each of the following sentences to make the helping verb part of a contraction.

1. She will make sandwiches for us.

____

2. You have done a good job.

____

3. He did not finish his homework.

____

4. They are traveling through Europe.

____

Name ______________________________

Compare Celebrations

Use information from the story and prior knowledge to compare the Mexican holiday *Día de los Muertos* (Day of the Dead) with Halloween as it is celebrated in the United States. Write words or phrases in the Venn diagram below that describe or relate to these holiday celebrations. You do not have to use complete sentences.

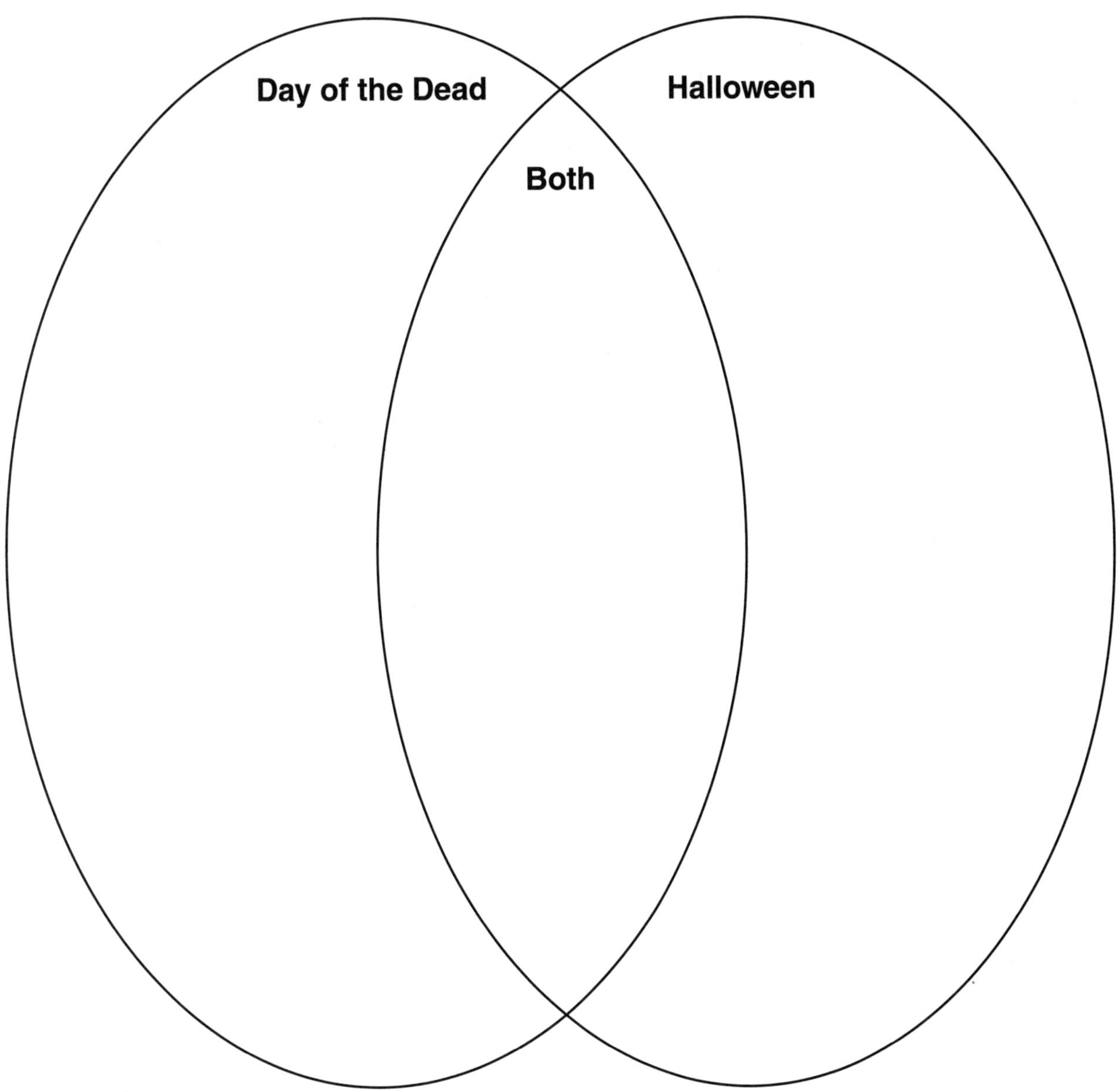

Comparing Texts

Along with building background and activating prior knowledge or experience, comparing texts is an important reading strategy that aids and improves reading comprehension. The focus of this reading strategy is making connections. In comparing texts, students make text-to-text connections based on what they read.

Comparing texts is a heavily tested reading objective that promotes both literary analysis and critical-thinking skills. By making text-to-text connections, students

- learn how to compare and contrast literary elements such as characters, plot, theme, and setting;
- better understand individual texts by seeing them juxtaposed with one another; and
- practice higher-order critical and creative thinking.

The activities on the following pages ask students to think about two stories and then answer questions that compare the texts. The activities are suitable for both group instruction and independent practice (see page 4). Before comparing the texts, students must have read both of the stories and should have completed some or all of their related skill pages.

Name ____________________

Two Sisters and *The Day Pecos Bill Rode Old Twister*

1. Answer the questions below to compare the conflict, or problem, for the main character in each story.

   a. What was the main problem for…

   Etta? ____________________

   Pecos Bill? ____________________

   b. What was the source of the problem for each character? Fill in the circle next to the correct answer.

   Etta: Ⓐ another person Ⓑ the environment Ⓒ herself

   Pecos Bill: Ⓐ another person Ⓑ the environment Ⓒ himself

   c. What characteristic, or trait, did each character use to deal with the problem?

   Etta: ____________________

   Pecos Bill: ____________________

   d. By solving the problem, what good did the character accomplish?

   Etta: ____________________

   Pecos Bill: ____________________

2. Choose **one** of the following adjectives: *big, clever,* or *determined.* Explain how the same adjective describes each character below.

   Etta: ____________________

   ____

   Pecos Bill: ____________________

   ____

3. Which story would you choose to perform as a play with your classmates? Why?

   ____

   ____

Name ____________________

America's First Lady of Courage and Picturing History

1. Which genre, or type of writing, are both stories an example of? Check the correct box.

   ☐ historical fiction ☐ autobiography ☐ biography ☐ fantasy

2. The phrases below describe one or both of the main characters in the stories. Write the letter for each phrase in the correct section of the Venn diagram.

   a. took risks
   b. had many assistants
   c. mastered five languages
   d. had one or more disabilities
   e. recorded historical events
   f. was a popular speaker
   g. was self-taught
   h. met famous and important people

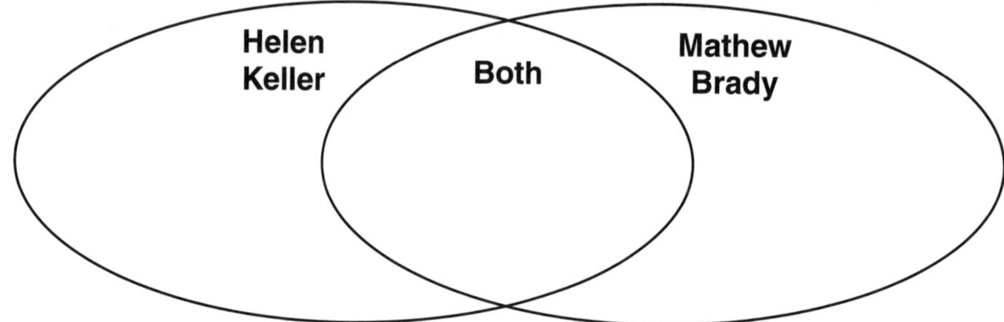

3. Contrast the kinds of books written by Helen Keller with those that Mathew Brady created.

   ____

   ____

4. What did each person do during his or her lifetime that was related to war?

   Helen Keller: ____________________

   Mathew Brady: ____________________

5. Explain how **both** Mathew Brady and Helen Keller...

   a. faced challenges. ____________________

   ____

   b. showed persistence. ____________________

   ____

Name ___________________________

Japanese Celebrations and *Let's Celebrate*

1. Write the title of each story on the line next to the correct genre, or type of writing.

   Fiction: ___________________________

   Nonfiction: ___________________________

2. Look for similar ways of celebrating holidays in both stories. Then complete the chart below. Write the name of a holiday on each line in the appropriate category.

Putting Up Displays	Giving or Eating Candy
___________ ___________ ___________	___________ ___________ ___________
Entertaining Visitors	**Watching or Being in Parades**
___________ ___________ ___________	___________ ___________

3. Check the box next to the correct answer.

   a. What is the author's purpose for writing *Japanese Celebrations*?

   ☐ to describe ☐ to instruct ☐ to persuade

   b. What is the author's purpose for writing *Let's Celebrate*?

   ☐ to instruct ☐ to persuade ☐ to entertain

4. How are the reasons for celebrating the Gion Festival and *Día de los Muertos* different?

   ____

   ____

   ____

Name ______________________

Comparing Texts

Nancy Lopez and Family and *Jackie Robinson*

1. Which description fits both stories? Fill in the circle next to the correct answer.
   Ⓐ sports biography
   Ⓑ autobiography of a champion
   Ⓒ historical fiction
   Ⓓ magazine article

2. Write one similarity and one difference between the childhoods of Nancy Lopez and Jackie Robinson.

   Similarity: ______________________

   ____

   Difference: ______________________

   ____

3. As young athletes, Lopez and Robinson experienced racial prejudice, but a particular event in each of their lives helped them overcome racial barriers. Answer the following questions about these events.

   a. What happened that helped Lopez play in golf competitions?

   ____

   ____

   b. What happened that helped Robinson play baseball in the major leagues?

   ____

   ____

4. Both Lopez and Robinson were ambitious. Name at least three other qualities they probably both had that helped them become such outstanding athletes.

   ____________ ____________ ____________

5. Both Lopez and Robinson had a lot of courage. Name at least one other quality they probably both had that helped them overcome discrimination.

   ____

Answer Key

Page 8

1. They are common foods for birds. The crow wanted something special (a delicacy) to eat.
2. Students who agree might say that the crow was able to steal the cheese without getting caught.

   Students who disagree might say that the crow was not able to hang onto the cheese after he stole it and that the fox was the clever one. They might also say that the farmer would have stopped the crow if the crow hadn't been able to fly away.
3. The fox did not seem to like the crow. The crow thought too well of himself and was too boastful.
4. Possible answers include:

   He strutted along his branch.

   He didn't want to eat common foods like the other crows.

   He purposely waited to eat so he could devour his treat in front of the other crows.

   He believed all of the fox's flattery.
5. The fox had flattered him into showing off his singing.
6. Answers will vary. Accept any reasonable suggestions.

Page 9

9, 5, 7, 2, 8, 1, 4, 6, 10, 3

1. imitate, spied, melodious, glisten, common, boast, serenade, pranced
2. wiliest, cunning, sliest

Page 10

Definitions will vary. Accept any that are reasonably accurate.

1. a. **dis**appear: to not be in view or to not be seen
   b. **re**place: to put in place again
   c. **fore**see: to see or realize something before it happens
   d. **mis**taken: accepted or believed in a wrong way
   e. **en**rich: to make more valuable or rewarding
2. a. patient
   b. polite
   c. unpleasant
   d. pleased
   e. uncommon
   f. incomparable

Page 11

1. Possible answers include: clever, can talk, uses flattery, scheming
2. Possible answers include: boastful, vain, choosy, sneaky, easily fooled, can talk
3. The crow has a flaw. He is vain.
4. The fox wants the crow's cheese.
5. Answers will vary but should include the idea that if you're too proud or vain, you could lose more than you gain.

Answers will vary. Possible answers include:

You have outfoxed the farmer.

I have never encountered a thief as clever as you are.

You are far more cunning than the sliest of us.

You are as handsome as you are clever.

Your feathers glisten in the sunlight; your eyes sparkle like jewels.

No creature in the forest can compare to you.

No one can imitate your soothing, melodious tones.

Every creature in the forest will enjoy your musical talent; I foresee a great musical future for you.

Page 15

1. Answers will vary but should include the idea of present-day gender equality. Accept any reasonable response.
2. He was grateful that his prayers had been answered and organized the parade to show his appreciation to the gods.
3. c, b, e, a, c, b, f, d
4. Answers will vary.

Page 16

1. l, d, j, f, i, h, k, c, a, e, g, b
2. Wording will vary but must convey the idea "seen from above," "seen from the air," or "looking down on."
3. Content of sentences will vary, but students must correctly identify the usage of each word as a noun or a verb.

Page 17

1. a. celebrate — tion
   b. happy — ness
   c. symbol — ize
   d. bright — ly
   e. courage — ous
   f. Japan — ese
   g. value — able
   h. music — ian
   i. thank — ful
2. a. ful
   b. able
   c. ness
   d. ese
   e. ing
   f. ly
   g. ian
   h. tion
   i. ous

Bonus: acting in a way that is full of care

Page 18

1. (circled words)
   a. tiered, red, special
   b. Greeting, family, New Year's, Japanese, traditional
   c. Some, bamboo, colorful, paper
2. a. strong, courageous (fish)
   b. brightly colored (carp kites)
   c. painted porcelain (faces)
   d. huge decorated (boxes)
   e. bare winter (trees)
   f. snow (and) ice (sculptures)
3. Adjectives will vary. Examples:
   a. tall brick (tower)
   b. lush green (meadow)
   c. shiny red (bicycle)
   d. warm wool (sweater)
   e. small china (vase)

Page 22

1. Answers will vary. Possible answers include:

   He was jealous of Jordan winning all the time.

   He didn't like Jordan's superior attitude.

   He didn't like the comments Jordan always made about how he should run the race if he wanted a better chance to win.

2. He ran his fastest from the start of the race and didn't have enough energy at the end to surge ahead of anyone who caught up with or passed him. Jordan paced himself earlier in the race and saved some energy for a burst of speed at the end of the race.
3. His grandfather, who as a young man had run in the Olympics, was coming to see the race. Also, Zach knew that his grandfather hoped he would run in the Olympics someday, too, and Zach had told his grandfather that he was the best runner on his team.
4. competing with yourself and trying to better your own record each time you run
5. No matter how fast you are, there will always be someone who can beat you to the finish line.
6. Answers will vary but should include the idea that he tried to place less importance on winning to let Zach know that, win or lose, he loved him and was proud of him. He also tried to show more interest in other activities, for both himself and for Zach. He seemed to realize that running had been too important even in his own life.

Page 23

1. a. competition, compete
   b. competitor
   c. competitive
2. a. challenging
   b. challenge
   c. challenger
3. a. congratulations
   b. congratulate
4. a. event
   b. eventful

Page 24

A. b, d, a, e, c, f

B. 1. noun
2. verb
3. verb
4. noun
5. noun
6. verb

C. Sentences will vary but *record* must be used as a noun in the first sentence and as a verb in the second sentence.

Examples:
Our school's top runner set a new state *record.* (noun)

During practice, our coach has to *record* the runners' finishing times in each event. (verb)

Page 25

Ideas for new endings will vary, but they all must include interaction between Zach and Jordan and a statement revealing Zach's feelings about the outcome of the race.

Page 29

1. a. They risk being caught and killed by the cat.
   b. They would have to flee for their lives and leave all their possessions behind to get past the cat, and they wouldn't know what new dangers they might have to face somewhere else.
2. Agatha's first suggestion was to ask the farmer's wife to leave food scraps for the mice. Her second suggestion was to move and find a place to live where the mice would be welcome.
3. Percy felt that Agatha didn't understand that the people in the house despise mice as much as the cat does and that the mice would be risking their lives if they tried to get past the cat to leave.
4. Percy risks his own life every day to feed his family. He also showed leadership ability by calling a meeting of the mice to try to find a solution to the cat problem.
5. The cat detected the mice and came after them in the closet, so Percy thought that climbing through the walls to the attic might be safer.
6. Answers will vary. Some students might be surprised that the mice were so enthusiastic about such a dangerous task. Some might not be surprised, because the mice didn't seem to think about how dangerous Leah's suggestion was before they responded.

Page 30

A.

1. prowl	7. frantic
2. gash	8. feline
3. utter	9. fond
4. collapsing	10. fanged
5. fiendish	11. lurks
6. sensibly	12. shudder

B. Sentences will vary. Examples:

1. I'll eat broccoli sometimes, but I despise spinach.
2. The big dog was snarling and showing its teeth, so I backed away slowly.
3. Our South African neighbors had to flee their homeland during the country's civil war.

Page 31

1. a. how to save the mice from being eaten by the cat
   b. how to get the mice out of her house
   c. how to catch the mice
2. a. The cat likes the farmer's wife. When she praises him and pets him, he purrs and snuggles in her arms.
   b. Percy doesn't trust people. He thinks they're selfish, and he knows they don't like mice.
   c. The farmer's wife thinks that the cat is clever and wonderful for catching so many mice.
3. a. She had seen that solution work with a barn cat she used to live with.
   b. No. Agatha said that Leah's solution was "very clever," but she knew that it was too dangerous to even try. She challenged the mice to volunteer for the job, knowing that none of them would.

Page 32

Answers will vary.

Page 35

1. Weeds absorb vitamins and minerals from the soil that are passed on to the animals that eat them.
2. a. roast them
   b. boil them to eat like spinach
   c. boil them to make tea

3. Decaying weeds deposit the calcium they have absorbed back into the soil, and when the soil is washed into a stream or river, algae and other water plants absorb the calcium. The fish that eat the plants take in the calcium and then pass it on to the people and animals that eat them.
4. Their roots hold the soil in place so the winds and heavy rains that cause erosion can't blow it or wash it away.
5. Fish and other water animals may die without the clean water they need.

   Food crops may be damaged by flooding.

   Hydroelectric power plants can't operate properly or may not work at all.
6. Most farmers don't like weeds because they are fast-growing plants that can quickly take over the fields and damage crops or keep them from growing. Weeds also absorb a lot of the water and nutrients that farm crops need.

Page 36

A. 5, 3, 10, 6, 4, 9, 2, 7, 1, 8

B.
1. deposit, nutrients
2. absorb
3. topsoil
4. sprout
5. erosion
6. sediment
7. calcium
8. decay

Page 37

A.

1. S	6. S
2. A	7. A
3. A	8. S
4. S	9. S
5. A	10. A

B.

1. ~~uncommon~~	common
2. ~~huge~~	microscopic
3. ~~worthless~~	valuable
4. ~~repair~~	damage
5. ~~tighten~~	loosen
6. ~~cause~~	prevent

Page 38

A. 1. Answers will vary. Possible answers include:

They are sources of food and nutrients for animals.

They enrich the soil.

They help prevent erosion.

They shelter small animals.

2. Answers should be similar to one of the following:

   They grow very quickly, last a long time, and can grow almost anywhere, even where most other plants cannot.

   Most people don't want weeds in their gardens because the weeds crowd out the garden plants and use up the water and nutrients in the soil that the other plants need.
3. Some humans cook the leaves of dandelions and chickweed and eat them like spinach. Humans also pick and roast dandelion flowers and boil the roots to make tea.
4. Answers should be similar to one of the following:

   Decaying weeds deposit calcium and other minerals and vitamins into the soil and break down to make new soil.

   The roots of weeds loosen the soil so that animals can dig and burrow more easily, and they hold the soil in place, which helps prevent erosion.
5. Answers should be similar to one of the following:

   Tall weeds slow down strong winds.

   Prickly weeds shelter small animals.

B. Opinions will vary but answers must include facts that support the opinions.

Page 41

1. when she was six years old
2. She learned new ways to control her voice.
3. In Europe, she was free to study music and languages without discrimination, and she was free to pursue her career with no limitations or restrictions. She was invited to sing in many countries, and her singing was praised openly.
4. African Americans were not allowed to perform there.
5. She was invited by the U.S. government to sing there, and her performance was attended by 75,000 people, both blacks and whites. This performance also led to an invitation to perform at the White House.
6. Answers will vary but should include reasons similar to the following:

   Because she was a performer who was known and admired throughout the world, the officials who appointed her to the UN delegation probably thought that she would represent America very favorably and had the ability to promote goodwill. Having lived, worked, and studied in Europe, she was already well-traveled and knew several different languages, and her concert tour through Southeast Asia had recently broadened her travel experience and probably made her as well-known there as she was in Europe and North America.
7. on Easter Sunday, 1965, at Carnegie Hall in New York City

Page 42

1. A	5. B
2. B	6. A
3. B	7. B
4. A	8. B

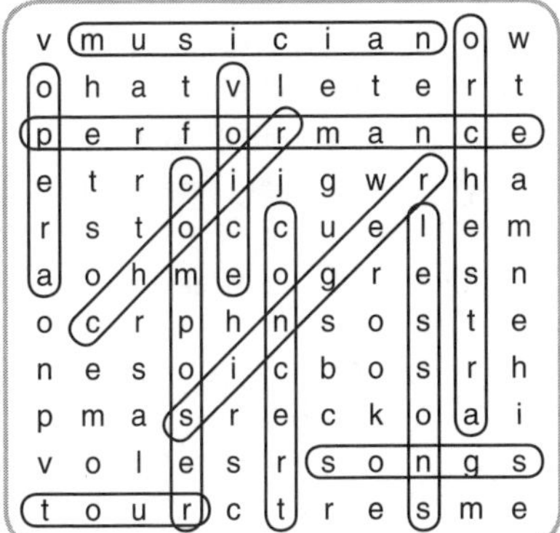

Page 43

A. **Childhood and Adolescence**

3, 2, 1, 4, 5

Early Career

5, 2, 1, 4, 3

Later Success

1, 3, 2, 4, 5

B. Answers will vary, but the events must be in chronological order.

Page 44

Answers will vary.

Example:

Talented

She began singing at age six and became known for her singing before she had finished high school.

Ambitious

She studied foreign languages so that she could sing in those languages in Europe.

Brave
She sang for 75,000 blacks and whites in front of the Lincoln Memorial at a time when black Americans were still heavily discriminated against.

Successful
She was the first African American singer to become a member of the New York Metropolitan Opera.

Page 48

1. 1776
2. The journey was too dangerous, and life in Alta California was difficult. Everyone had to work very hard; they had no comforts and few supplies, and they had to do and make everything for themselves.
3. He was responsible for the fields and the cattle while his father was guarding the mission and the community.
4. Answers may vary, but the most probable is that they were not able to read and write.
5. Yes. He kept the caravan moving in spite of terrible hardships. He also cared for the sick and did his best to keep everyone cheerful and hopeful.
6. Possible answers include:

   organizing the large caravan each day

   finding food and water for the animals

   surviving windy, dusty, and bitter-cold conditions

   crossing deserts, and wide, rushing rivers

   losing animals that strayed off or could not survive the harsh conditions

   finding shelter and wood for fires
7. The letter has to be taken to New Spain by ship and then carried along with other mail and supplies by mule train.

Page 49

1. Adobe
2. galleon
3. caravan
4. hardships
5. Alkali
6. despondent
7. Comforts
8. Fording

1. our family
2. Juan Bautista de Anza
3. the Pimas
4. animals
5. native people
6. soldiers
7. galleon
8. message

Page 50

Sentences will vary, but they must convey the meaning of each word accurately.

Page 51

Sequencing: 6, 4, 8, 5, 2, 7, 3, 1

Generalizing: Answers will vary. Possible answers include:

1. In the 1700s, few people traveled from New Spain to Alta California because the journey, by land or sea, was difficult and dangerous.
2. People probably braved the hardships to travel from New Spain to Alta California because they wanted to be the first settlers there and hoped to find rich land for farms and ranches.

Page 54

1. No one knows who built the city or even what language its inhabitants spoke.
2. The Aztecs named the city. The name means "city of the gods."
3. Rising 200 feet (61 meters) in the air, it is as tall as a 20-story building, and it covers about 500,000 square feet (46,450 sq m) of ground.
4. In that era, people probably didn't know about metals or how to make things from metals, so they used stone instead.
5. Answers will vary. Possible answers include:

   The city was conquered and destroyed by enemies and the people were killed or captured, with any survivors scattering to other places in search of safety.

   The city and its people were wiped out by disease or natural disasters.
6. Answers will vary.

Page 55

A. 9, 3, 7, 10, 8, 5, 4, 1, 6, 2

B.

1. scattered
2. murals
3. system
4. marketplace
5. incense
6. ceramic

Page 56

1. not in the earth
2. a person who sells or trades things
3. a person or thing who inhabits or lives in a place
4. not integrated, combined, or together
5. a person who studies science
6. a person who studies or works with archaeology, or the objects and structures of ancient times
7. to do the opposite of hide or cover
8. a person who travels
9. a person who studies people and their cultures
10. a person who resides, or lives, at a certain place

Page 57

Answers will vary.

Page 60

1. Because a doctor had told Nancy's mother to exercise regularly, her parents played golf every day. Nancy was only eight years old, so she had to go along. When she got bored, she asked if she could play, too, and her father helped her get started.
2. 13 years (She started playing golf at age 8 and turned pro at age 21.)
3. Her school had no girls' golf team, and she had to get help from a lawyer before she could join the school's boys' team.

   Because Nancy was a Mexican American, the local country club (in Roswell) didn't want to sponsor her so she could enter competitions. She was fortunate, however, that a country club in Albuquerque saw sponsoring her as an opportunity.
4. She had taken some time off from golf and may have been a little out of practice. She also still thought about her mom a lot and may have had difficulty concentrating on her game.

5. Answers may include any two of the following:

   She had been a champion golfer from a very young age and as an adult, shattered golf records and won many awards and competitions.

   She was warm, cheerful, and friendly to everyone.

   She broke racial barriers and boundaries for both Mexican Americans and women in professional golf.
6. The author wanted the reader to understand the importance of Nancy's family in her life and to realize how much her parents helped her and what they sacrificed so that she could compete and enjoy her success.

Page 61

course, sand traps, clubs, hole, stroke, tournaments, amateur, professional, rookie, sponsor

Page 62

1. E: she started playing golf, too.
2. E: Nancy could practice hitting a golf ball out of the sand.
3. C: playing in golf tournaments was expensive.
4. E: Nancy asked to join the boys' golf team
5. C: her high school would not let her play on the boys' team.
6. E: a country club in Albuquerque made Nancy and her family honorary members.
7. E: she earned money playing golf.
8. C: she won a lot of tournaments and broke a lot of records, and she was a warm and friendly person.

Page 63

Answers will vary.

Page 67

1. Someone left the iguana at the pet store where Martin's Aunt Belle worked. The pet store couldn't keep it, so she gave it to Martin as a birthday present.
2. a. the garden
   b. other apartments
   c. the laundry room
   d. the parking lot
   e. the garbage cans
3. He remembered that iguanas always head for a warm place, and the basket of laundry Aunt Mary had taken to her sister was warm, right out of the dryer.
4. She'd probably never expect to find a real lizard in her laundry basket, and she had been sick, so she might not have been very alert. Also, Iggie probably sat motionless on top of the warm television.
5. Answers will vary but should include most of the following facts:

   Aunt Mary is pleasant, friendly, and helpful. Everyone calls her "Aunt" even though she isn't related to them. She invited the boys into her apartment and did whatever she could to help Martin find Iggie. She also helped her sister, who was sick. She is good-natured and seems able to laugh easily about things, such as her sister's reaction to Iggie.

Page 68

					c	o	n	v	i	n	c	e			
											h				
	z							s	t	r	e	t	c	h	
	o		v	a	n	i	s	h			c			o	
p	o	k	e					r			k			l	
	m		n		a	r	r	i	v	e				l	
			t					e				b		e	
	s		u		j	e	r	k			w	o	r	r	y
	u		r									r			
	g	u	e	s	s				s	e	a	r	c	h	
	g			e		m			h			o			h
	e			t		u			a			w	a	v	e
	s				k	n	o	c	k						a
	t					c			e						d
						h									

Page 69

1. full-grown
2. spiny
3. scaly
4. motionless

1. Iggie is an iguana, which is a large reptile with spines down its back.
2. Maintenance workers are around dirt and garbage on the job and wear gloves to protect their hands.
3. Iguanas like warm places, and the sun warms the surface of a parking lot during the day.
4. She thought that Iggie was a toy, so he must have had a power source to move.
5. Aunt Belle is Martin's guardian, so she needs to approve of where he goes and who he's with.
6. Clean clothes right out of the dryer make a nice, warm bed.
7. Iguanas like to eat larvae.

Page 70

Headlines and details will vary, but the headlines must be accurate and the details must be in the story.

Example:

Beginning: Lizard Vanishes

1. Martin can't find his pet iguana, Iggie, anywhere.
2. Martin knows that iguanas need to stay warm, and he's worried that his pet will be out in the cold all night.

Middle: Boys Search for Lost Iguana

1. Martin and his friend Arnold look for Iggie in every warm place they can think of.
2. Martin puts a bowl of mealworms outside the front door, hoping that Iggie will come home looking for food.

End: Martin Finds Iggie

1. Aunt Mary's sister finds Iggie in the basket of laundry Aunt Mary returned to her, but she thinks the lizard is a stuffed toy.
2. Martin remembers Aunt Mary talking about the basket of laundry, convinces Aunt Mary to take him to her sister's to look for Iggie, and surprises Aunt Mary's sister by showing her that Iggie is a real, live lizard, not a toy.

Page 74

1. He couldn't go to school with white children or play with his white neighbors, and he was called hateful names.
2. She peacefully protested the mistreatment of blacks on city buses by staying in her seat on the bus and appealing her arrest in court.
3. King felt that blacks should stand up for their rights but in peaceful, nonviolent ways.
4. Answers will vary but should include the following ideas:

   Marches are a peaceful way to bring people together to support each other, to get the attention of law enforcement officials and government representatives, and to show the will of the people.
5. The March on Washington probably convinced legislators of the need and the public's desire for the prompt creation and enforcement of a new Civil Rights Act.

6. Answers will vary. Possible answers include:

   hateful attitudes

   unjust laws or failure to enforce laws that protect citizens' rights

   convincing blacks to protest in nonviolent ways

   dealing with threats and violence against himself, his family, and other African Americans

Page 75

A. Examples will vary. Possible examples include the following:

1. **P** injustice: Black citizens who registered to vote were threatened or harmed.
2. **S** sit-ins: Blacks sat in seats reserved for whites on buses and in restaurants and theaters to protest segregation.
3. **P** mistreatment: Marchers were attacked by police dogs and blasted with water from fire hoses.
4. **S** boycotts: Blacks did not ride the buses in Montgomery, Alabama, to protest having to sit in the back of the bus and being expected to give up their seats to white people.
5. **S** integration: After a year of boycotting the buses in Montgomery, Alabama, black people were given the same rights as white people to sit in any seat.

B. f, h, d, a, c, b, e, g

Page 76

A. Answers will vary but should include some of the following ideas:

He helped bring about justice and equality for all people.

He taught people to care about each other and live in harmony.

He encouraged people not to give up on their dreams.

He gave the people eloquent and encouraging speeches that are known and repeated throughout the world.

He showed people the power of love and how to fight violence with love.

He showed people how to bring about reform without violence.

B. Answers will vary.

Page 77

Answers will vary. Possible answers include the following:

Brave

He preached and taught others peace and love in spite of enduring racial injustices all his life.

He made himself responsible for millions of others by leading a massive movement to correct injustices.

He was true to his belief in nonviolent reform even when he and his family were threatened and attacked.

He served as president of the SCLC, which was an organization that peacefully opposed unjust laws.

He gave his life for his dream of equality and civil justice for all.

Influential

He united hundreds of thousands of people in a massive civil rights movement.

He persuaded his followers to fight injustice without violence.

He organized and led peaceful protests such as marches and sit-ins.

He was an eloquent and persuasive speaker, whose words are still remembered and quoted throughout the world.

His efforts led to Congress passing the Civil Rights Act of 1964.

Peace-Loving

He did not believe that anger and violence would solve the problems of injustice.

He became a minister and a church pastor to teach others to believe in in the power of peace and love. He insisted on peaceful protests and persuaded his followers to repay injustices with love.

He was awarded the 1964 Nobel Peace Prize.

Unselfish

He put the needs of others before his own comfort and safety.

He worked tirelessly to correct injustices and to promote civil rights for all people.

He gave up his life for his cause and for the people he tried to help.

He defined the dream of justice, not only for African Americans but for everyone.

Page 81

1. They are able to move quickly; they can gallop up to 35 miles (56 km) per hour.

   They are very tall and have good eyesight, so they can see trouble coming over a mile (km) away.

   They have strong hooves that can badly injure an attacker.

   The patterns of their coats make young giraffes easy to hide in tall grass and other natural surroundings.

   They watch out for each other, especially when a group is drinking at a watering place.

2. Answers can be any four of the following:

   They weigh between 1,800 and 3,000 pounds (816 and 1,360 kg).

   The average height of females is 14 to 16 feet (4.25 to 5 m).

   The average height of males is 16 to 18 feet (5 to 5.5 m).

   They can walk up to 10 miles (16 km) per hour or gallop up to 35 (56 km) per hour.

   Their necks are 6 to 8 feet (2 to 2.5 m) long.

   When it's pointed straight up, a giraffe's head adds 2 feet (61 cm) to its height.

   A giraffe's heart is about 2 feet (61 cm) long and weighs about 24 pounds (11 kg).

   A giraffe's tongue is about 18 inches (46 cm) long.

   A newborn calf is about 6.5 feet (2 m) tall.

   A giraffe can see something more than a mile (km) away.

3. Other animals know that giraffes can see predators or problems that are over a mile (km) away.
4. Oxpeckers help keep giraffes clean. They walk along a giraffe's back, eating insects and getting rid of dry skin and loose hair. Giraffes provide food (insects) for the oxpeckers.
5. Humans are taking over more and more of the land in the giraffes' habitats. Humans are also killing giraffes for food, hides, and tail hair.

6. Because tourists want to see giraffes and other wild animals, the Africans try to protect the animals. Tourists need food and lodging, which provides jobs for Africans, and the money that tourists spend also helps Africa and its people.

Page 82

A.

1. sheltered
2. droughts
3. shift
4. unique
5. ruminants
6. irregular
7. cud
8. joint
9. digest
10. preserve
11. valves
12. arteries

B.

1. tourists
2. gallop
3. ranchers
4. moisture

Page 83

A.

1. with a long neck
2. to its neck
3. of acacia trees
4. into its mouth
5. from many countries

B. There are many possible answers. You may want to have students look for each other's answers in the story.

Page 84

I. A. can see something moving over a mile (km) away

B. Other animals at watering places depend on them to spot danger.

II. A. Each pattern is different.

B. Some have spots that are close together with straight edges.

C. Some have irregular spots.

D. Colors of spots vary.

III. A. have stomachs with four sections

B. swallow food whole

C. bring up swallowed food to chew and swallow again

D. Food is digested in the fourth section of the stomach.

IV. A giraffe does not bathe.

Page 88

1. Etta's land was hilly, dry, and rocky with no water nearby. Gretta's land had fields and orchards planted on it and was near a stream.
2. She removed rocks, terraced the hills, and cultivated the soil, and when there wasn't enough rain, she walked to the river to get water for the plants.
3. Gretta thought that Etta was using magic.
4. Gretta thought that she was growing more fruit because she had found out Etta's magic words and was saying them to the apple tree every day.
5. Etta tried to teach Gretta how to take care of her trees. She didn't try to get back any of the trees Gretta had stolen and even brought Gretta more new trees and planted them for her. Etta also explained what the "magic" really was and showed Gretta what she needed to do to make her trees grow successfully.
6. Etta meant that the growing process was amazing (magical) and the produce was tantalizing and delicious (enchanting), but it was not magic (enchanted).

Page 89

A.

1. sturdy
2. enchanted
3. inherited
4. terracing
5. cultivating
6. confronted
7. worthless
8. orchards
9. prosperous
10. complain

B. Answers may be any six of the words listed for each group.

plants: apple, blossoms, branches, crops, fields, fruit, leaves, orchard, pears, produce, roots, tree, vegetables, weeds

farm work: cultivating, dig, grow, harvested, planted/planting, producing, prune, replant, terracing, trim, water

Page 90

1. A	5. B	9. B
2. A	6. B	10. A
3. B	7. A	11. B
4. A	8. B	12. A

Page 91

Possible answers include:

Etta

satisfied
grateful
hardworking
kind
helpful
cared for her crops
didn't complain
made the most of things
clever

Gretta

dissatisfied
ungrateful
envious
careless
didn't like working for anything
liked to feel important
complained a lot
sneaky
dishonest
a thief

Both

inherited land
had an orchard
grew crops
wanted to be successful

Page 94

1. C
2. Answers may be any three of the following:

   chasing barn cats

   stomping in cow pies

   throwing each other into haystacks

   taking the little kids for wheelbarrow rides

   letting the little kids kiss the cows
3. All of the noise and activity the children generated probably frightened the farm animals and made them uncomfortable.
4. The author sat quietly in a corner near the adults and listened to their conversations.
5. I loved Sunday afternoons in summer.

   I was the most reluctant to say goodbye to another Indiana Sunday.
6. Answers will vary but must include a reasonable explanation.

Page 95

3, 11, 2, 5, 10, 8, 12, 6, 4, 1, 7, 9

dinner — lunch
porch — recreation room
cellar — basement
brood — family
womenfolk — women
nook and cranny — corner or small space

Page 96

Answers will vary but should be similar to the following:

1. The adults stopped talking about them but would resume the discussion at another time.
2. The children were kicked (sent) out of the basement.

3. They realized that it was getting late in the day, and it was time go home and start thinking about Monday morning.

1. Answers will vary. Accept any clearly expressive phrases or sentences from the story.

   Examples:
   the loud ringing of the huge bell
   The cows mooed their complaints.
   clamored into the mosquito-free house
   battle with cue sticks
   found a corner on the floor of the adult world
   The door squeaked open.
   adult talk slowed with each disappearing brood
2. a tractor

Page 97

1. corn
2. Illinois, Indiana, Iowa, Michigan, Minnesota, North Dakota, Wisconsin
3. North Dakota
4. Kansas, Nebraska, South Dakota
5. Michigan, Wisconsin
6. Missouri, Ohio

Page 100

1. Helen had severe disabilities herself. She was both blind and deaf and was unable to communicate effectively. As a young girl, she was frustrated and angry with her inability to communicate, so her behavior was often out of control, and she had a lot of temper tantrums.
2. They probably weren't upset because, when she thanked them, she had asked to use the money to help another child. The people knew she was grateful, and they were probably proud of her for being so generous and unselfish with the money.
3. Annie Sullivan was such an important part of Helen's life that Helen probably wrote the book *Teacher* to honor Annie and let others know how special she was.
4. It took an incredible amount of determination and hard work for Helen to accomplish all the things she did, but she did not let her disabilities stand in her way. She was also very generous in helping others, especially those with disabilities, to live full lives and to treat each other with dignity.
5. Answers will vary but should include any three of the following:

   She graduated college with honors.
   She mastered five languages.
   She traveled throughout the world.
   She met many famous and important people.
   She wrote books.
   She worked for foundations, raising money and supporting laws to help the disadvantaged and disabled.
   She spoke to crowds of people and visited soldiers blinded in WWII, spreading encouragement and hope to people everywhere.

Page 101

1. stroke
2. mastered
3. pantry
4. disabled
5. fragile
6. commission
7. traced
8. dignity
9. tutor
10. foundation
11. tantrum
12. Braille

1. count
2. assist
3. early
4. fame
5. graduate
6. accomplish
7. advantage
8. organize

Page 102

Answers will vary. Examples:

1. Pretend you're knocking on a door.
2. Imitate turning a steering wheel.
3. Pretend you're opening a book.
4. Pretend you're conducting an orchestra.
5. Pretend you're winding a reel of film in an old movie camera.
6. Smile and pretend you're waving to your friend.
7. Pretend you're bouncing and then shooting a basketball into the air.
8. Pretend you're counting out money.
9. Pretend you're taking an exam or raising your hand in class.
10. Pretend you're holding a glass up to your mouth and swallowing.

Page 103

Answers will vary.

Page 107

1. He howled like a coyote to make the cattle stampede and stationed cowpunchers along the trail to keep them moving in the right direction.
2. He was raised by coyotes and, until he was fourteen, he thought that he was a coyote.
3. He could smell it and hear it.
4. He threw a rope over it, climbed on top, and rode it like a bucking bronco.
5. The twister was getting uglier by the minute.
6. He scooped them out of the twister and dropped them onto the ground to make a town where people traveling west could stop and rest.
7. It tired itself out and turned into a gentle breeze.

Page 108

			b													
	s	t	a	m	p	e	d	e	d					b		
	i		r								c			r		
	d		e			f	r	i	n	g	e	d		o		
	e		b			r					l			n		
	s	t	a	t	i	o	n	e	d		l			c		
	t		c			l				l	a	s	s	o		
	e		k			i					r		p			
	p					c							o			
	p					k		b	u	n	k	h	o	u	s	e
	i		t			i		o					k		p	
	n		w	r	a	n	g	l	e	r			e		u	
	g		i			g		t					d		r	
			s					e							s	
p	a	n	t	h	e	r		d								
			e													
	s	t	r	e	t	c	h									

Page 109

1. as truthful as a Sunday school teacher
2. as tall as a two-story house
3. like the points on a picket fence
4. like blades of brown prairie grass
5. as calm as a hibernatin' bear
6. like a buckin' bronco at a rodeo
7. as gentle as a newborn lamb frolickin' across a meadow
8. like an angry panther chasin' its dinner

Page 110

Answers will vary. Possible answers include the following:

Pecos Bill was as tall as a two-story house. *No person is that tall.*

Coyotes raised him. *Animals don't raise human children.*

Bill could smell almost anything in the air a hundred miles away. *No one can smell anything that far away.*

Bill put his ear to the ground and announced, "It [the twister] just passed by El Paso. It's an hour away." *You can't hear where or how far away a storm is by listening to the ground.*

… into the tunnel Bill had dug using his pet snake, Rattler, as a drill. *A snake can't be used to dig or drill.*

When the twister caught sight of Bill, it set out after him. *A storm doesn't go after a particular person or place.*

Bill led Old Twister away from the barn. *No one can control the path or direction of a storm.*

Old Twister wasn't used to playin' a losin' game of tag. *A storm can't think and doesn't play games.*

Bill sent his rope whirling faster than a bolt of lightnin'. *No one can twirl a rope that fast.*

The lasso dropped over the top of Old Twister… he [Bill] jumped onto the side of the twister and climbed toward the top… *A person cannot rope [lasso], ride, put spurs into, fight with, or control a storm.*

Bill reached down inside the whirlwind and pulled out the houses one by one… *No one can take objects, big or small, out of a tornado, and no one can create a town by tossing or dropping houses, plants, and animals onto the ground.*

Page 113

1. Artists painted their portraits.
2. Possible answers include:

   The process took a long time, and the subject had to sit without moving for up to 30 minutes.

   The plate had to be exposed to light at just the right time and for just the right amount of time and then quickly covered again.

   The photographer had to develop the picture in dim candlelight.

   The picture was very delicate and had to be placed in a glass case for protection.

   If the picture didn't turn out or was damaged during processing, there was no way to fix it.
3. Because he took thousands of pictures right on the battlefields and in army camps, he could be considered a photojournalist, reporting the faces and facts of the war in pictures.
4. People at that time didn't want to be reminded of the war.
5. His photographs of presidents and other famous people show what they really looked like, and his pictures of Civil War battles and soldiers provided and preserved a visual historical record of the war.
6. Answers will vary. Possible answers include: digital photography, instant photo printing, the ease of altering photographs electronically, storing images on disks and in computers

Page 114

A. 1. portrait
2. restore
3. image
4. mercury
5. plate
6. daguerreotypes
7. studio
8. preserve
9. darkroom
10. carted
11. exposed
12. evict

B. 1. fixed A
2. solution B

Page 115

A. 2. Expose the plate to iodine vapors to make it light-sensitive.

4. Let the image "burn" onto the surface of the plate.
5. Cover the plate quickly.
6. Take the plate into a darkroom.
8. Fix the image with a salt solution.
9. Put the image inside a glass box to protect it.

B. 1830 Daguerreotypes were being made in France.

1844 Brady opened his New York City photography studio and began making daguerreotypes.

1850 Brady opened another studio in Washington, D.C.

1861 Brady photographed Civil War battles.

1871 The government agreed to buy 2,000 portraits from Brady but never made the purchase.

1881 Brady had to close the Washington, D.C., studio.

1896 Brady died.

Page 116

1. Brady learned how to make daguerreotypes.
2. Brady worked by dim candlelight in a darkroom.
3. Brady started the process all over again.
4. Brady hired assistants and opened a second studio.
5. Brady and his assistants carted all of his equipment and his darkroom to the photo site.
6. Brady tried to sell the photos to the government so he could pay his debts and save his business.

Answers will vary.

Page 119

1. He spent a lot of his time working to help out his family.
2. Robinson left UCLA in 1941, shortly before the attack on Pearl Harbor, and was drafted by the army in 1942. Also, at that time, black athletes weren't allowed to play on major league sports teams.
3. Answers may be any three of the following:

   He was the first black player in major league baseball.

   He was the first black player voted into baseball's Hall of Fame.

   He was the first player in major league sports to have his uniform number retired from all major league baseball teams.

   He was the first black to become vice president of a major American corporation.
4. Answers should include at least two of the following:

   He raised money for the NAACP and served on its board for many years.

   He helped start Freedom National Bank.

   He started a construction company to build houses for low-income families.

   As a successful businessman and the first black to be vice president of a major American corporation, he was a positive and successful role model for other black Americans.
5. October 15, 1972, was the twenty-fifth anniversary of Robinson's first game in the major leagues. He was honored with a plaque that day, and he also threw out the first pitch for the second game of the 1972 World Series.

   November 15, 1997, was the day that all of major league baseball retired Robinson's uniform number (42).

Page 120

5, 3, 7, 1, 6, 2, 8, 4

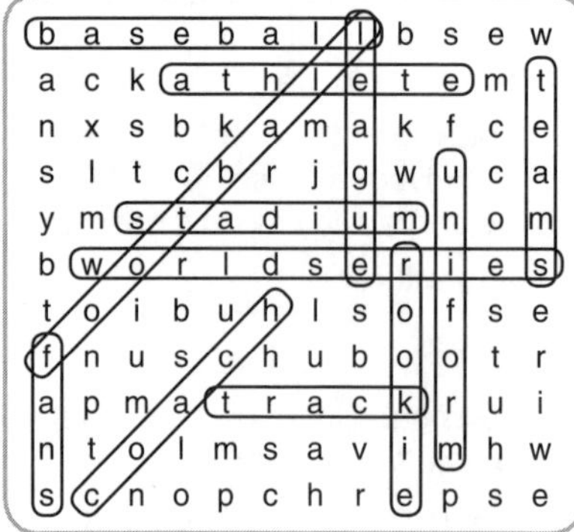

1. athlete
2. baseball
3. coach
4. fans
5. football
6. league
7. rookie
8. stadium
9. teams
10. track
11. uniform
12. world series

Page 121

A. Answers will vary but should be similar to the following:

1. a required period of time spent in military service
2. to introduce a new or different standard of action or behavior that makes something easier for others later on

B. 1. stopped working at a regular job or profession

2. took out of use

Answers will vary but should include the idea that many people still weren't in favor of having a black player in the major leagues, so Robinson had to face being disliked and probably ridiculed on almost a daily basis and had to tolerate or stand up to the people who were against him.

Page 122

Answers will vary. Possible answers include the following:

I. Childhood
(any 3 of the following)

born in Georgia in 1919

youngest of five children

family moved to Pasadena, California, when he was six months old

poor family

delivered newspapers, ran errands, cut lawns, and did other jobs to earn money to help his family

II. High School and College
(any 2 of the following)

played four sports (baseball, basketball, football, track)

went to UCLA

first college athlete to win awards in four sports

III. Sports Career
(any 4 of the following)

assistant athletic director for a youth program

athletic coach in the army (not allowed to play on army baseball and football teams)

played football

coached basketball

played baseball for Kansas City Monarchs (Negro American League)

played minor league baseball for the Montreal Royals

played major league baseball for the Brooklyn Dodgers

IV. Business Career
(any 3 of the following)

successful businessman

was a board member and raised money for the NAACP

helped found Freedom National Bank (owned and operated by black Americans)

started a construction company to build houses for low-income families

vice president of a major corporation

V. Awards and Honors
(any 4 of the following)

first black player in modern major league baseball

major league baseball's Rookie of the Year (1947)

major league baseball's Most Valuable Player (1949)

first black player in baseball's Hall of Fame

uniform number retired by the Brooklyn Dodgers (1972)

plaque commemorating 25th anniversary of his first game in the major leagues

threw out first pitch at second game of the 1972 world series

uniform number retired by all of major league baseball (1997)

Page 126

1. The cocoa beans used to make chocolate come from the pods of cacao trees.
2. on the trunk
3. Cacao pods ripen in 5 to 6 months, and they are purple when they are ripe.
4. Answers should be "no" unless students live in one of the tropical zones near the equator.
5. a mixture of seasonings and corn mash and sometimes honey, vanilla, and chili peppers
6. sugar, orange water, white rose powder, cloves, and other spices
7. A nib is the inside of a cocoa bean. Roasted nibs are crushed to release cocoa butter, and then the cocoa butter is removed in different amounts to make different types of chocolate paste.
8. Answers will vary.

Page 127

A. 1. pods
2. plantations
3. tropical
4. aromatic
5. drizzle
6. caffeine
7. survey

B. Sentences will vary. Examples:

1. Cacao trees are **native** to Mexico.
2. Cacoa trees grow best in **zones** near the **equator**.
3. Cocoa beans are inside **cacao** pods.
4. They are **harvested** and the seeds and **pulp** are removed.
5. It has a **tantalizing** smell.

Page 128

A. Adjectives will vary. Examples:

Taste: nutty, fruity, tangy, bitter, salty, bittersweet, smokey

Texture: smooth, gooey, moist, mushy, creamy, crunchy

B. Drawings, ingredients, and descriptions will vary.

Page 129

Answers should be similar to the following but can be in any order within each section.

1. a. Cacao trees grow in tropical zones near the equator.

   b. Cocoa beans are inside the pods that grow on the trunks of cacao trees.

c. When cacao pods are harvested, the cocoa beans are removed.

d. After the bitter cocoa beans are dried, they have the sweet smell of chocolate.

2. a. Dried cocoa beans are sent to candy factories.

b. The beans are roasted and the nibs are crushed.

c. Different amounts of cocoa butter are removed from the crushed nibs to make different types of chocolate paste.

d. Various ingredients are added to chocolate paste to make different flavors and types of chocolate products.

3. a. The Aztecs used chocolate to make a special drink.

b. Spanish explorers brought chocolate to Spain and made their own special chocolate drink.

c. Visitors to Spain took the chocolate drink back to their own countries, and chocolate became popular throughout Europe.

d. In the 1700s, chocolate was shipped from England to the British colonists in North America.

4. a. Chocolate is a good source of minerals, vitamin B, and energy.

b. Like coffee, chocolate contains caffeine, which often keeps people awake when they need to rest.

c. Because chocolate contains fat and calories, most people should eat it only occasionally.

d. Chocolate is very popular throughout the world.

Page 133

1. They helped him develop his passion for books by reading to him and having him read to them. Because they felt that education was important, they made sure that Laurence had enough time to study, even if it meant not being able to work as much in their grocery store. The sandbox that Mr. Yep built also helped stimulate Laurence's imagination for creating fantasy kingdoms.
2. His mother was born and raised in America, and his family did not live in Chinatown or near many other Chinese American families. They also didn't practice a lot of Chinese traditions on a daily basis, and Laurence did not speak Chinese as well as other Chinese Americans his age.
3. His favorite books were fantasy, especially books about Oz, and he also liked science fiction. He felt a lot like the characters in these books, who were thrust into strange worlds where they didn't belong, which was how he felt about being Chinese and American.
4. When he didn't do well in his college journalism classes, a teacher suggested that he might be better at writing fiction than reporting facts.
5. *Sweetwater.* Joanne Ryder, a student he had known in college, became a children's book editor for a New York publisher and asked him to write it and send it to her.
6. *Dragonwings* (1975) and *Dragon's Gate* (1993)

Page 134

3, 6, 8, 5, 1, 4, 2, 7

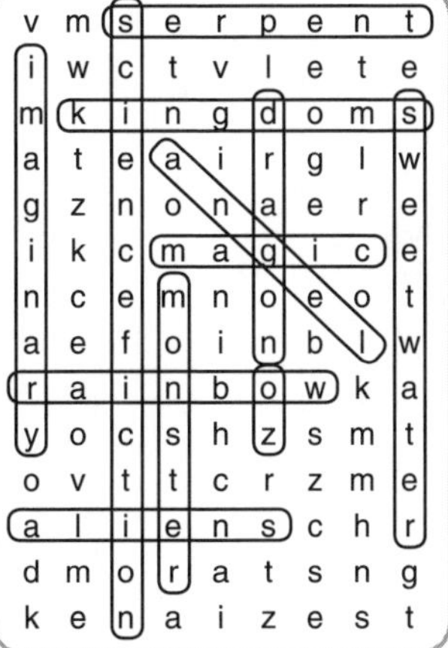

v	m	s	e	r	p	e	n	t
i	w	c	t	v	l	e	t	e
m	k	i	n	g	d	o	m	s
a	t	e	a	i	r	g	l	w
g	z	n	o	n	a	e	r	e
i	k	c	m	a	g	i	c	e
n	c	e	m	n	o	e	o	t
a	e	f	o	i	n	b	l	w
r	a	i	n	b	o	w	k	a
y	o	c	s	h	z	s	m	t
o	v	t	t	c	r	z	m	e
a	l	i	e	n	s	c	h	r
d	m	o	r	a	t	s	n	g
k	e	n	a	i	z	e	s	t

Page 135

A. Questions will vary but should be well thought out and pertinent.

B. Answers will vary.

Page 136

Kingdoms and descriptions will vary.

Page 140

1. to go to school and to practice speaking English
2. Lisa thought that she'd have to spend a lot of time helping Elena with her homework and wouldn't have time to visit friends, watch TV, or do anything fun. Also, her mother had told her that she couldn't be in the school play.
3. Lisa convinced her mom that Elena should be in the play, so she could learn about American holidays and practice speaking English at the same time.
4. They invited the souls of their ancestors to visit and cleaned up the cemetery and decorated it with flowers for them. They also set up a home altar with candles and pictures of their ancestors and put out special foods at the cemetery and at home to welcome the spirits of the dead.
5. Answers will vary but should include the idea that people want to remember their loved ones and any other people who were important in their lives.

   In the United States, Memorial Day is the national holiday that honors all those who have died defending and protecting the country.

Page 141

1. souls
2. cemetery
3. pleaded
4. cabinet
5. rehearsals
6. acquainted
7. altar
8. honor
9. insisted
10. arrange

1. evening
2. forgotten
3. strange
4. emptied
5. friends
6. downstairs
7. together
8. honor
9. followed
10. smiled
11. arriving
12. opened

Page 142

A. Action Verb	**Helping Verb**
1. come	had
2. bringing	is
3. give	can
4. miss	will
5. hoping	was

B. 1. **She'll** make sandwiches for us.
2. **You've** done a good job.
3. He **didn't** finish his homework.
4. **They're** traveling through Europe.

Page 143

Answers will vary. Possible answers include the following:

The Day of the Dead

candles	ancestors
pictures	*pan de muertos*
altar	flowers
food	

Halloween

costumes	spiders/webs
parties	trick-or-treating
witches	carving pumpkins
black cats	jack-o'-lanterns
bats	bobbing for apples

Both

bones	end of October
cemetery	spirits (ghosts)
skeletons	candy
skulls	

Page 145

1. a. Etta: keeping her sister, Gretta, from taking trees from her orchard

   Pecos Bill: keeping a twister from destroying his ranch

   b. Etta: A

   Pecos Bill: B

   c. Etta: cleverness or kindness

   Pecos Bill: physical strength or courage

   d. Etta: She taught her sister how to grow and care for her own trees.

   Pecos Bill: He saved everyone in the area from a tornado and created a new town for travelers.

2. Answers will vary. Example: Etta: She was **determined** to help her sister become successful at growing things.

   Pecos Bill: He was **determined** to stop the twister.

3. Answers will vary. Accept any reasonable explanation for the student's story choice.

Page 146

1. biography
2. Helen Keller: c, f
   Mathew Brady: b, e, g
   Both: a, d, h
3. Helen Keller wrote her own autobiography as well as a biography of her teacher Annie Sullivan.

   Mathew Brady preserved history by creating the story of the Civil War in pictures.
4. Helen Keller visited soldiers who were blinded in battles during WWII.

   Mathew Brady risked his life to take photographs in army camps and on battlefields during the Civil War.
5. a. Helen Keller overcame the limitations of being both blind and deaf.

   Mathew Brady taught himself the complex, time-consuming process of making photo portraits and then improved the process.

   b. Once Helen Keller had learned about language, she eagerly kept learning until she had mastered five languages and had become a world-famous speaker.

   Mathew Brady continued taking photographs in spite of his failing eyesight, having his equipment destroyed on a Civil War battlefield, and being unable to sell his pictures.

Page 147

1. Fiction: *Let's Celebrate*
   Nonfiction: *Japanese Celebrations*
2. **Displays** (any 3 of the following):
   Children's Day
   Hina Matsuri
   Tanabata
   Sapporo Snow Festival
   Day of the Dead
   (Día de los Muertos)

   Candy
   Shichi-Go-San
   Halloween
   Day of the Dead
   (Día de los Muertos)

   Visitors
   Hina Matsuri
   New Year's Day
   Day of the Dead
   (Día de los Muertos)

   Parades
   Gion Festival
   Cinco de Mayo
3. a. to describe
   b. to entertain
4. The Gion Festival gives thanks for lives that were saved. The Day of the Dead honors ancestors who have died.

Page 148

1. A
2. Similarity: Lopez and Robinson were both from minority families that didn't have much money.

   Difference: Even as a young boy, Robinson had to work to help support his family and didn't have time for sports until high school. Lopez began playing golf at the age of 8 and was already competing at the age of 12.
3. a. In order to play competitive golf, Lopez needed a sponsor. When the local country club in Roswell refused to sponsor a Mexican American family, a country club in Albuquerque was happy to make the Lopez family honorary members.

   b. When major league baseball teams still hired only white ballplayers, Branch Rickey, the president of the Brooklyn Dodgers, boldly signed Robinson to play on the Dodgers' minor league team, the Montreal Royals. A year later, Rickey signed Robinson to play for the Dodgers in the major leagues.
4. Answers will vary. Possible answers include: skillful, strong, confident, talented, focused, determined, competitive
5. Answers will vary. Possible answers include: patient, calm, forgiving, tolerant, understanding, even-tempered